BOLLINGEN SERIES LVII

JOLANDE JACOBI

Complex / Archetype / Symbol

IN THE PSYCHOLOGY OF

C. G. JUNG

TRANSLATED FROM THE GERMAN BY

RALPH MANHEIM

BOLLINGEN SERIES LVII

PRINCETON UNIVERSITY PRESS

Copyright © 1959 by Bollingen Foundation Inc., New York, N.Y.
Published by Princeton University Press

THIS IS THE FIFTY-SEVENTH IN A SERIES OF WORKS
SPONSORED BY BOLLINGEN FOUNDATION

Originally published in German as
*Komplex / Archetypus / Symbol
in der Psychologie C. G. Jungs*
by Rascher Verlag, Zurich and Stuttgart, 1957

Library of Congress Catalogue Card No. 59-9185
ISBN 0-691-01774-3 (paperback edn.)
ISBN 0-691-09720-8 (hardcover edn.)

First PRINCETON / BOLLINGEN PAPERBACK Edition, 1971

Third Printing, 1974

Princeton University Press books are printed on
acid-free paper and meet the guidelines for permanence
and durability of the Committee on Production
Guidelines for Book Longevity of the Council
on Library Resources

Manufactured in the United States of America

14   13   12   11

CONTENTS

v

II. ARCHETYPE AND DREAM

CONTENTS

ILLUSTRATIONS

FOREWORD[1]

The problem this book is concerned with is one in which I, too, have been interested for a long time. It is now exactly fifty years since I learned, thanks to the association experiment, the role which complexes play in our conscious life. The thing that most impressed me was the peculiar autonomy the complexes display as compared with the other contents of consciousness. Whereas the latter are under the control of the will, coming or going at its command, complexes either force themselves on our consciousness by breaking through its inhibiting effect, or else, just as suddenly, they obstinately resist our conscious intention to reproduce them. Complexes have not only an obsessive, but very often a possessive, character, behaving like imps and giving rise to all sorts of annoying, ridiculous, and revealing actions, slips of the tongue, and falsifications of memory and judgment. They cut across the adapted performance of consciousness.

It was not difficult to see that while complexes owe their relative autonomy to their emotional nature, their expression is always dependent on a network of associations grouped round a center charged with affect. The central emotion generally proved to be individually acquired, and therefore an exclusively personal matter. Increasing experience showed, however, that the complexes are not infinitely variable, but mostly belong to definite categories, which soon began to acquire their popular, and by now hackneyed, designations—inferiority complex, power complex,

[1] Translated by R. F. C. Hull.

ix

father complex, mother complex, anxiety complex, and all the rest. This fact, that there are well-characterized and easily recognizable types of complex, suggests that they rest on equally typical foundations, that is, on emotional aptitudes or *instincts*. In human beings instincts express themselves in the form of unreflected, involuntary fantasy images, attitudes, and actions, which bear an inner resemblance to one another and yet are identical with the instinctive reactions specific of *Homo sapiens*. They have a dynamic and a formal aspect. Their formal aspect expresses itself, among other things, in fantasy images that are surprisingly alike and can be found practically everywhere and at all epochs, as might have been expected. Like the instincts, these images have a relatively autonomous character; that is to say they are "numinous" and can be found above all in the realm of numinous or religious ideas.

For reasons that I cannot enter into here, I have chosen the term "archetype" for this formal aspect of the instinct. Dr. Jacobi has made it her task, in this book, to expound the important connection on the one hand between the individual complex and the universal, instinctual archetype, and on the other hand between this and the symbol. The appearance of her study is the more welcome to me in that the concept of the archetype has given rise to the greatest misunderstandings and—if one may judge by the adverse criticisms—must be presumed to be very difficult to comprehend. Anyone, therefore, who has misgivings on this score can seek information in this volume, which also takes account of much of the literature. My critics, with but few exceptions, usually do not take the trouble to read over what I have to say on the subject, but impute to me, among other things, the opinion that the archetype

INTRODUCTION

The present period is characterized by a terminological tower of Babel. This is particularly true in the field of psychology, this youngest of the sciences, and perhaps most of all in the branch that has been termed "depth psychology."[1] As the sciences split into more and more numerous specialized branches, the available vocabulary has been unable to keep pace with the differentiation of concepts. Even in related disciplines, insurmountable terminological difficulties have brought about constant misunderstandings. Depth psychology, which is equally indebted to the natural and the humane sciences, is far from having perfected an appropriate vocabulary of its own, and its literature is full of foreign implantations. The very nature of depth psychology prevents it from adopting a procedure which is both possible and desirable in mathematics and physics, and which has been attempted by the positivists and logisticians in the field of philosophy,[2] namely the creation of an "intersubjective language" consisting of word signs of invariable meaning. It has still to "purify" its terminology from the overdetermined "residua" inherited from mythological tradition as well as physics, medicine, and other disciplines with which it was

[1] Strictly speaking, the term "depth psychology" should be applied only to Freud's "psychoanalysis" and Jung's "analytical psychology." But the term is loosely used for all those schools which in their theoretical and practical work attach fundamental importance to the hypothesis of the "unconscious."

[2] Attempts in this direction have been made, for example, by such philosophers as Ludwig Wittgenstein and Bertrand Russell.

formerly linked. At the same time it must contend with an often impenetrable tangle of polyvalent psychic phenomena and, in perfecting its nomenclature, do justice to the laws of the inner cosmos, lest it fall a victim to a doctrinaire systematization—an all but impossible task.

Narrow, one-sided formulations kill the life of the psyche, whose mobile, dual face, seamed with paradoxes, refuses to such endeavors its secret, which can never be captured by strict conceptual methods. Its essence remains forever ambivalent and evades all efforts to unveil it. Yet, says Jung, it is "the only immediate experience we can have and the *sine qua non* of the subjective reality of the world."[3] Thus in the last analysis any attempt to formulate psychic phenomena in terms of language is doomed to imperfection, because the means of expression can never be fully adequate to the subject matter. And the more stratified, profound, and comprehensive become the psychic phenomena dealt with, and the greater the reality, the autonomy—not to mention the immateriality—that we ascribe to the psyche, the more acutely will this discrepancy be felt. On the other hand, it will be less apparent where the field to be considered is more limited, more closely related to the world of the senses and of matter—where the psychic world is regarded as mere epiphenomenon. From their own standpoint, accordingly, the stanch champions of a strict psychophysical parallelism cannot be blamed for refusing the label of "science" to the aspect of depth psychology that cannot be verified by controllable experiments and expressed in unambiguous concepts. Yet this is only one more indication that all attitudes, particularly in psychology, are primarily sub-

[3] *Symbols of Transformation*, p. 232.

4

jective. For every statement on psychic phenomena is more crucially influenced by the personal position of the man who makes it, and by the spirit of the age that molds him, than is the case in other scientific fields. Nowhere else is it so evident that the "personal equation" which begins at the moment of observation is carried over into the linguistic expression and conceptual crystallization.

In view of all this, it is not surprising that misunderstandings and misinterpretations should abound in the field of depth psychology, often leading to sterile polemics. It is equally understandable that a desire should be felt on all sides to remedy this situation. In the present work I have endeavored to clarify and illuminate (though without going into a detailed history of their development) three basic concepts of Jung's vast intellectual edifice—concepts that have given rise to numerous misunderstandings. In view of the considerations set forth above, such a venture cannot hope for complete success. A venture it is and remains. I should like it to be regarded as a contribution toward the "common language" that is so much to be desired, and not as a definitive statement.

COMPLEX

The feeling-toned groups of representations in the unconscious

According to Jung,[1] it is not dreams (as Freud believed) but complexes[2] that provide the royal road to the unconscious. These words indicate the dominant, the central role that he assigns to the complex in depth psychology. The term itself, to be sure, is also used currently to denote all sorts of "composite structures," but it has found its most important application in the field of depth psychology. Eugen Bleuler (1857–1939) had already used it to designate certain psychic conditions, but it is Jung who defined it in the sense accepted today. In his exhaustive studies at the Psychiatric Clinic of the University of Zurich, published under the title *Diagnostische Assoziationsstudien*,[3] he first applied the term "feeling-toned complex" to the phenomenon of the "feeling-toned groups of representations" in the unconscious; later the term was shortened to "complex."

Still wholly on the basis of the experimental psychology of the consciousness, and with the help of its methods, Jung and his coworkers conducted a series of tests which

[1] Jung came to this conclusion on the basis of his observations in the course of his experiments on the process of association. He noted that the "complex-indicators" not only provide a direct proof of the existence of an unconscious realm of the psyche, but also provide information regarding its hidden contents and their emotional charge.

[2] "A Review of the Complex Theory" (C. W. 8), par. 210.

[3] *Studies in Word Association* (tr. by M. D. Eder). [C. W. 2.]

indicated the presence and nature of such emotionally toned groups of representations as specific factors disturbing the normal course of the psychic association process. The point of departure was the associative process as a reflection of psychic activity. It was shown by carefully conducted experiments that the "disturbances" in question are of an intrapsychic nature and originate in a realm which is beyond the objective control of the conscious mind and which manifests itself only when the threshold of attention is lowered.[4] This not only provided new proof of the existence of an unconscious realm whose manifestations would have to be taken into account in any psychological statement, but also offered the possibility of observing its workings directly and investigating them by experiment.[5] In the association test—which cannot here be discussed in detail—it was shown that the speed and the quality of the reactions to "stimulus words" selected in accordance with a definite principle are individually conditioned. A prolonged reaction time when the subject is first exposed to the stimulus, and the faults (gaps or falsifications of memory) occurring when the subject attempts to recall during a repetition of the experiment the answers given through spontaneous association, are not accidental but are determined with incredible precision by the disturbing effects of unconscious contents sensitive to the action of

[4] The various "disturbances" of the associative process have also been studied experimentally by other methods, such as pulse and respiration curves, measurements of resistance to electric currents (in which the so-called "phenomenon of the psychogalvanic reflex" first explored by Veraguth provided valuable information), etc.

[5] On the basis of his experiments in hypnotism and his method of dream analysis Freud came to the same conclusion. The symptomatic actions first described by him, the "disturbances" of the psychic process, which, in neurotic states, appear in the form of symptoms, correspond to the "complex-indicators" verified by Jung in his association experiments.

a complex. The nature and duration of the symptoms of disturbance consequently permit inferences as to the feeling tone and depth of the affect-laden contents concealed in the background of the psyche.

"The entire mass of memories," writes Jung of his experience of an emotional complex, "has a definite feeling tone, a lively feeling [of irritation, anger, etc.]. Every molecule [of the complex] participates in this feeling tone, so that, whether it appears by itself or in conjunction with others, it always carries this feeling tone with it, and it does this with the greater distinctness the more we can see its connection with the complex-situation as a whole." Jung adds in a footnote: "This behavior might be compared to Wagnerian music. The leitmotiv, as a sort of feeling tone, denotes a complex of ideas which is essential to the dramatic structure. Each time one or the other complex is stimulated by something someone does or says, the relevant leitmotiv is sounded in one of its variants. It is exactly the same in ordinary psychic life: the leitmotivs are the feeling tones of our complexes, our actions and moods are modulations of the leitmotivs." And in another: "The individual representations are combined according to the different laws of association (similarity, coexistence, etc.), but are selected and grouped into larger combinations by an affect."[6]

According to Jung's definition every complex consists primarily of a "nuclear element," a vehicle of meaning, which is beyond the realm of the conscious will, unconscious and uncontrollable; and secondarily, of a number of associations connected with the nuclear element, stem-

[6] *Über die Psychologie der Dementia praecox*, p. 44. "[The Psychology of Dementia Praecox," C. W. 3, here tr. R.F.C.H. Cf. Brill tr., pp. 34-35 and notes.]

ming in part from innate personal disposition and in part from individual experiences conditioned by the environment.[7] Supposing we take an image of the "paternal," of the Greek god Zeus, for example, in an individual's unconscious as such a "nuclear element." We can speak of a "father complex" in this individual only if the clash between reality and the individual's own vulnerable disposition in this respect, the clash between the particular inward and outward situations,[8] gives this "nuclear element" a sufficiently high emotional charge to carry it out of a state of merely "potential" disturbance into one of actual disturbance. Once constellated and actualized, the complex can openly resist the intentions of the ego consciousness, shatter its unity, split off from it, and act as an "animated foreign body in the sphere of consciousness."[9] Accordingly Jung says: "Everyone knows nowadays that people 'have complexes'; what is not so well known . . . is that complexes can *have us*."[10] And yet this is the crucial point on which we must gain clarity if we are to counter the prevailing smug faith in the supremacy of the will and of ego-consciousness with the doubt it deserves.

Autonomy of the complexes

Complexes may disclose every degree of independence. Some rest peacefully, embedded in the general fabric of the unconscious, and scarcely make themselves noticed; others behave as real disturbers of the psychic "economy";

[7] Cf. Jacobi, *The Psychology of C. G. Jung* (London, 1951), pp. 51 ff.; (New Haven, 1951), pp. 45 ff.

[8] "A Psychological Theory of Types," in *Modern Man in Search of a Soul*, p. 92. [C. W. 6.]

[9] "A Review of the Complex Theory," par. 201.

[10] Ibid., par. 200.

still others have already made their way into consciousness, but resist its influence and remain more or less independent, a law unto themselves.

"The ego complex," writes Jung, "forms the center characteristic of our psyche. But it is only one among several
complexes. The others are more often than not associated
with the ego complex and in this way become conscious, but
they can exist for some time without being associated with
the ego complex."[11] They lurk as it were in the background
of the unconscious until a suitable constellation calls them
to the plane of consciousness. Then they often act in-
visibly, inwardly preparing the way for some transformation. For the conscious mind may be aware of the presence of a complex—how frequently we hear sufferers
from psychic disorder saying: "I know that I have a
mother complex," etc.—and yet, not knowing the underlying causes, be unable to resolve it. Knowledge of its existence seems futile; its harmful action will continue until
we succeed in "discharging" it, or until the excess of
psychic energy stored up in it is transferred to another
gradient, i.e., until we succeed in assimilating it emotionally.

These complexes, that are only intellectually known,
must be sharply distinguished from those that are really
"understood," i.e., made conscious in a form that actually
stops them from exerting a harmful influence. For in these
latter cases we are no longer dealing with complexes but
with assimilated contents of consciousness as, for example,
in the case of a mother complex that has ceased to be one,
because it has been resolved and its content transformed
into a natural relation to the mother. Still, it must be

[11] "The Psychological Foundations of Belief in Spirits" (C. W. 8),
par. 582.

stressed that once we become consciously aware of a complex, it has a better chance of being "understood" and corrected, i.e., made to disappear, than if we have no suspicion of its existence. For as long as it remains totally unconscious and the attention of our consciousness is not attracted to it even by the symptoms it causes, it remains inaccessible to any possible understanding. It then possesses the uncontrollable, compulsive character of all autonomous forces to which the ego is exposed for better or worse; it promotes dissociations and so impairs the unity of the psyche.

Jung points out expressly that as long as complexes are unconscious they can be enriched with associations and hence "broadened," but can never be corrected. They cast off the compulsive character of an automatism only when we raise them to consciousness, a step which is among the most important elements of therapy. In proportion to their distance from consciousness, the complexes take on in the unconscious an archaic-mythological character and an increasing numinosity through enrichment of their contents, as can easily be observed in cases of schizophrenia. But numinosity is totally impervious to the conscious will and puts the subject into a state of seizure, of will-less subservience. The conscious complexes, on the other hand, can be corrected and transformed. They "slough off their mythological envelope, and, by entering into the adaptive process going forward in consciousness, they personalize and rationalize themselves to the point where a dialectical discussion becomes possible."[12]

From the functional point of view we may say that the resolution of a complex and its emotional assimilation, i.e.,

[12] "On the Nature of the Psyche" (C. W. 8), par. 384.

the process of raising it to consciousness, always result in a new distribution of psychic energy. For the psychic energy that has been held fast in the complex can then flow off into new contents, and so bring about a new situation more propitious to psychic balance.

Thus the complexes are impressive indicators not only of the "divisibility" or "dissociability" of the psyche but also of the relative independence of the fragments, which may amount to complete psychic disintegration in all its variants.[13] This fact, which is a primordial experience of mankind, is the basis of the view, widespread particularly among primitive peoples, that several souls can coexist in one and the same person. "Fundamentally," says Jung, "there is no difference in principle between a fragmentary personality and a complex," for complexes are often "splinter psyches."[14]

Thus the complex—as is clearly shown by dreams—may appear in personified form. And the same observation can be made in spiritualistic manifestations, automatic writing, and such phenomena. For dream images "enter like another kind of reality into the field of consciousness of the dream ego. . . . They are not subject to our control but obey their own laws. They are . . . autonomous psychic complexes, which have the power to form themselves out of their own material."[15] The same is true of visions, hallucinations, and obsessions. A complex that has become autonomous can carry on a totally separate existence in the background of the psyche; it "forms, so to speak, a miniature self-contained psyche"[16] within the "big" psyche, and in certain psychotic states an autonomous complex

---

[13] Ibid., pars. 365ff.   [14] "Complex Theory," par. 202.
[15] "Belief in Spirits," par. 580.
[16] *The Practice of Psychotherapy*, par. 125.

can even draw attention to itself by a personal "voice" of its own.[17] The pronouncements of mediums in states of trance are always expressed in the first person, just as though a real individual were speaking. In his doctoral dissertation, "On the Psychology and Pathology of So-called Occult Phenomena," Jung pointed out such mani-festations in the trance states of mediums and character-ized them as "attempts of a future personality (whose partial aspects they represent) to break through."

Since the autonomous complexes are by nature un-conscious, they seem—like all manifestations of the un-conscious—not to belong to the ego, i.e., to be qualities of outside objects or persons, in other words, *projections*. Notions of persecution, the belief in "spirits," based on such projections, or the phenomenon of possession com-mon in the Middle Ages (in which the ego is totally "swallowed up" by the complex, because the complex proves even more powerful than the ego complex)[18] may be interpreted as a "direct expression of the complex structure of the unconscious." But whether "such small psychic fragments as complexes are capable of a con-sciousness of their own is still an unanswered question."[19]

[17] Excellent examples of this are provided by Ludwig Stauden-maier, *Die Magie als experimentelle Naturwissenschaft* (1912) and Aldous Huxley, *The Devils of Loudun* (1952).

[18] Jung interprets the ego "as a reflection, not of one, but of very many processes and their interplay—in fact, of all those processes and contents that make up ego-consciousness. Their diversity does indeed form a unity, because their relation to consciousness acts as a sort of gravitational force drawing the various parts together, towards what might be called a virtual center. For this reason, I do not speak simply of *the* ego but of an *ego complex*, on the proven assumption that the ego, having a fluctuating composi-tion, is changeable and therefore cannot be simply *the* ego." ("Spirit and Life" [C. W. 8], par. 611.)

[19] "Complex Theory," par. 202. Jung assumes the existence in the

However, certain experiences in the field of psychopathology—for example, the phenomenon of "dual personality"described by Janet—suggest that the existence of quasi-conscious processes in the unconscious must be considered at least as a possibility. At all events, complexes are "psychic agencies whose deepest nature is still unfathomed."[20] We can break their power only by "making conscious" their repressed and unconscious contents. This usually meets with strong resistance on the part of the patient and requires the specific method of "analysis"—unless an experience of grace or some form of catastrophe or hardship provides a shock sufficient to resolve the complex. Intellectual understanding is by no means sufficient. Only emotional experience liberates; it alone can bring about the necessary revolution and transformation of energies. No phenomenon of the unconscious can be apprehended by the intellect alone, "for [the complex] consists not only of *meaning* but also of *value,* and this depends on the intensity of the accompanying feeling tones,"[21] which in turn determine the role that the complex will play in the economy of the psyche.

"It is through the 'affect,' " Jung writes, "that the subject becomes involved and so comes to feel the whole weight of reality. The difference amounts roughly to that between a severe illness which one reads about in a text book and the real illness which one has. In psychology one possesses nothing unless one has experienced it in reality. Hence a purely intellectual insight is not enough, because one knows only the words and not the substance of the thing from inside."[22]

---

unconscious of *scintillae,* or seeds of light, i.e., germs of consciousness. Cf. "On the Nature of the Psyche," pars. 388ff.

[20] "Complex Theory," par. 216.   [21] *Aion,* par. 52.
[22] Ibid., par. 61.

On the phenomenology of the complex

The phenomenology of the complex reveals a wide diversity of forms. All of them may show somatic as well as psychic symptoms, and combinations of the two. We may briefly differentiate the following forms:

a) The complex is unconscious but not yet sufficiently charged with energy to be experienced as an "independent will," an autonomous entity; still, it more or less blocks the natural psychic process. It has preserved a relative connection with the totality of the psychic organization (e.g., it is manifested only in slips or other trifling symptoms).

b) The complex is unconscious, but already so "swollen" and independent that it acts as a second ego in conflict with the conscious ego, thus placing the individual between two truths, two conflicting streams of will, and threatening to tear him in two (as, for example, in certain forms of compulsion neurosis).

c) The "complex ego" can break completely out of the psychic organization, split off and become autonomous. This leads to the well-known phenomenon of "dual personality" (Janet), or to a disintegration into several partial personalities according to the number and nature of the patient's unconscious complexes.

d) If the complex is so heavily charged as to draw the conscious ego into its sphere, overpower and engulf it, then the complex has to a greater or lesser degree become ruler in the house of the conscious ego; then we may speak of a partial or total *identification* between the ego and the complex. This phenomenon can be clearly observed in men having a mother complex or women having a father complex. Unbeknownst to them, the words, opinions, desires, and strivings of the mother or father have taken possession of their ego, making it their instrument and mouthpiece. Such identity between complex and ego can of course vary in degree; it may cover only parts or the whole of the ego. In the former case, difficulties of adaptation, a relative loss of reality, psychic disorders of greater or lesser intensity will result; in the second case the unmistakable characteristics of a disastrous inflation will be manifested, as may occur, for example, in individuals who identify themselves with God or the devil, with a child or a goblin, with political or historical figures, or all manner of animals, and in the various forms of psychosis involving partial or total loss of the ego.

e) Since unconscious contents are experienced only in projected form, the unconscious complex appears first in projection as an attribute of an outward object or person. If the unconscious complex is so markedly "split off" as to take on the character of an entity (often of a menacing nature) assailing the individual from outside, or if it appears as an attribute of an object of outward reality, such symptoms occur as may be observed in persecution mania, paranoia, etc. This object may either belong to the actual outside world, or it may merely be thought to come from outside but actually stems from within, from the psyche. Such "objects" may take the form of spirits, sounds, animals, figures, etc.

f) The complex is known to the conscious mind, but known only intellectually and hence retains all its original force. Only the emotional experience coupled with the understanding and integration of its content can resolve it.[23]

The inability to distinguish between contents of the conscious mind and those stemming from the unconscious

[23] Cf. pp. 23ff., below.

complex, which "becloud" consciousness—as is always the case in d) and e)—constitutes a great danger; it prevents the individual from properly adapting himself to his inward and outward reality; it impairs his ability to form clear judgments, and above all thwarts any satisfactory human contact. This phenomenon of "participation," i.e., deficient ability to distinguish between subject and object, is often observed not only in neurotics but also in the primitive peoples who practice animistic religions, in small children, and in many adults who have remained in high degree unconscious. It is the psychic situation toward which the various propaganda techniques are directed. The stronger the tendency to "participation," that is to say, the less able the ego is to assert itself over against inundation by inward or outward psychic influences, the more readily will the individual be colored by, or succumb to, the spirit of a group, and become one with the mass. Maturity implies that the different parts of the psyche are recognized as such and brought into the proper relation to one another. In order to arrive at a harmonious interaction of these parts of the psyche, one must first of all distinguish and delimit them from one another. This makes it possible to keep the influences and incursions of the unconscious entirely separated from those that have already been clarified by consciousness—the two will no longer be confused. Ability to discriminate between them is therefore the prerequisite not only of a well-defined ego, but also, in the last analysis, of any higher culture.

Accordingly the ego can take four different attitudes toward the complex: total unconsciousness of its existence, identification, projection, or confrontation. But only confrontation can help the ego to come to grips with the complex and lead to its resolution.

The neurotic individual fears nothing so much as encounter with his inward and outward reality; for this reason he prefers to think life rather than to experience it. Often he shows an almost inconceivable attachment to his complexes, even when he seems to suffer unbearably from them and to do everything in his power to get rid of them. For something in him knows full well that no complex can be resolved unless one faces the conflict that causes it, and this requires courage, strength, and an ego that is capable of suffering. Often the individual must reconcile himself to unalterable facts of a negative or conflicting character. To abandon one's infantile fixations and adapt oneself to responsible adulthood is a severe trial and not at all what most people expect of analysis and of the resolution of their complexes. It is not an immersion in a state of "happiness." For if a complex has been made conscious, the hitherto unconscious conflict that has led to it becomes manifest. In order to sidestep the incompatibility between the two poles of the conflict, the individual has more or less consciously repressed and cut off one of them; he has seemingly got rid of it. In this way he has avoided suffering from the actual conflict, but in exchange he suffers from a pseudo problem, namely from all sorts of neurotic disorders and symptoms. The moral or ethical conflict at the root of the complex has seemingly been done away with, or rather, transposed to a plane on which one is, in a manner of speaking, "innocent"; it may, for example, be "displaced" to the bodily sphere, as in hysteria. One of the most frequent causes of complexes is indeed the so-called "moral conflict," i.e., apparent inability to affirm the whole of one's nature.

The difference between the conceptions of Jung and of Freud

Up to this point Jung's opinions and definitions in regard to the complex coincide with those of Freud.[24] But from here on Jung's conception differs *fundamentally* from Freud's, and this divergence has had vast consequences for the development of his whole doctrine. The failure to take this cleavage sufficiently into account has been one of the chief reasons for the misconceptions that have impeded a proper understanding of Jung's view.

Freud and Jung arrived, by entirely different paths, at similar conclusions regarding the nature and effects of the psychic factors known as "complexes." It was this agreement that first (1902) called their attention to one another and later (1907) brought them together for a time. By 1913 Jung had developed a fundamentally different view of the problem[25] and their ways parted. Jung had come to draw a sharp distinction between a "personal unconscious" (corresponding to the Freudian concept of the unconscious, whose contents consist exclusively of discarded or repressed material deriving from individual experience) and a "collective unconscious" (consisting of

[24] It seems to me that my attempt to explain this concept will be facilitated by a comparison between the views of Jung and of Freud, because the Freudian views are already widely known, particularly in academic circles.

[25] Jung first set forth his new approach in his fundamental work *Wandlungen und Symbole der Libido*, which appeared in 1912. Since then it has been (1952) reworked and published under the title *Symbole der Wandlung* (*Symbols of Transformation*, C. W. 5).

the typical patterns of human experience and behavior, i.e., of the "inherited potentiality of psychic functioning pure and simple").[26] In accordance with this theory, Jung attributed a wider significance and function to the "complexes." For him they became "focal or nodal points of psychic life, which *must not be absent*, because if they were, psychic activity would come to a standstill."[27] They constitute those "neuralgic points" in the psychic structure, to which undigested, inacceptable elements, elements of conflict, will cling, but "the fact that they are painful is no proof of pathological disturbance." All human beings have complexes. They constitute the structure of the unconscious part of the psyche and are its normal manifestations. "Suffering is not an illness; it is the normal counterpole to happiness. A complex becomes pathological only when we think we have not got it."[28]

We see that Freud and Jung came finally to a fundamentally different view, a totally different evaluation, of the complex. Freud saw the complex *only* as a manifestation of illness, Jung as pertaining also to a healthy human being. In Freud complexes always have a negative character; they are products of the psychic mechanism of repression, which in this way seeks to evade the conflict between the primitive sexual urges of man and the moral and social constraints

[26] "I fully agree with Jung," Freud writes, "in recognizing the existence of this phylogenetic heritage; but I regard it as a methodological error to seize on a phylogenetic explanation before the ontogenetic possibilities have been exhausted. I cannot see any reason for obstinately disputing the importance of infantile prehistory while at the same time freely acknowledging the importance of ancestral prehistory. . . ." (*From the History of an Infantile Neurosis* [Standard Edition, Vol. 17], p. 97.)

[27] "A Psychological Theory of Types," in *Modern Man in Search of a Soul*, p. 91 (mod.). [C. W. 6.]

[28] Cf. *The Practice of Psychotherapy*, p. 78, par. 179.

imposed on him, and are without exception symptomatic of a disturbed instinctual life, a diseased psyche. To bring them to awareness, i.e., to resolve them by raising their contents to consciousness with the help of the analytic method, is therefore desirable from the standpoint of therapy. To bring them fully to the surface (and thus empty the unconscious of all its contents) is perfectly possible in principle, though not in practice. Although he admits that the constitutional factor plays a certain role, Freud holds that every complex is inseparably linked with the individual's private life and rooted in the emotional experiences of his earliest years—which have become unconscious and split off, or have been repressed, because they are incompatible with the habitual state of consciousness.

Jung takes a different view: "Complexes obviously represent a kind of inferiority in the broadest sense—a statement I must at once qualify by saying that to have complexes does not necessarily indicate inferiority. It only means that something incompatible, unassimilated, and conflicting exists—perhaps as an obstacle, but also as a stimulus to greater effort, and so, perhaps, as an opening to new possibilities of achievement."[29]

Here Jung's teleological approach becomes evident: Evil can always be regarded as the starting point for good, sickness as a source of more intensive striving for health. Accordingly the complex may take on a positive, prospective significance. Thus for Jung one and the same complex has a dual aspect. He does justice to the Freudian aspect but goes beyond it and adds another. Since 1926 Jung's theory of the complex has developed greatly. At that time he still declared: "Experience shows us that complexes are infinitely varied, yet careful comparison reveals a rela-

[29] "A Psychological Theory of Types," p. 91.

tively small number of typical primary patterns, all of which have their origins in the first experiences of childhood."[30] Today Jung holds that certain complexes stem entirely from an actual situation, above all those which appear in the spiritual crises of middle life.

The two kinds of complexes

But Jung goes further and says:

"Many complexes are split off from consciousness because the latter preferred to get rid of them by repression. But there are *others that have never been in consciousness before*,[31] and therefore could never have been arbitrarily repressed. They grow out of the unconscious and invade the conscious mind with their weird and unassailable convictions and impulses."[32]

Does this mean that there are two kinds of complexes— those of the sick and those of the normal psyche, i.e., "morbid" and "healthy" complexes? Clearly this inference cannot be rejected, especially if we consider the passage quoted below and recall that Jung draws a certain distinction between the complexes of the personal unconscious and those of the collective unconscious.

"Certain complexes," he writes, "arise on account of painful or distressing experiences in a person's life. . . . These produce unconscious complexes of a personal nature. . . . But there are others [autonomous complexes] that come from quite a different source. . . . At bottom they have to do with irrational contents of which the individual had never been conscious before, and which he therefore

[30] Ibid., p. 92.
[31] Italics mine.—J.J.
[32] "Psychology and Religion" (C. W. 11), par. 22.

vainly seeks to discover somewhere outside him."[33] Or: "While the contents of the personal unconscious are felt as belonging to one's own psyche, the contents of the collective unconscious seem alien, as if they came from outside. The reintegration of a personal complex has the effect of release and often of healing,[34] whereas the invasion of a complex from the collective unconscious is a very disagreeable and even dangerous phenomenon. The parallel with the primitive belief in souls and spirits is obvious: souls correspond to the autonomous complexes of the personal unconscious, and spirits to those of the collective unconscious."[35]

Jung himself owns that in this connection his "theory of complexes" must strike the uninitiated as a "description of primitive demonology and of the psychology of taboos," and this is not surprising in view of the fact that the complexes are basically "vestiges of a primitive state of mind." But whereas Freud holds that by making them conscious it is possible to overcome this primitive (and hence infantile) state of mind completely and thus free the individual's psyche from its complexes, Jung believes that even the most extensive conscious realization can bring to the surface and resolve only a part of the complexes—namely, those which happen to be constellated. Whether for therapeutic purposes an attempt is made to free an individual from his psychic or psychogenic disorders; whether for pedagogic and social purposes a better adaptation to his environment is sought; or whether a profound transformation of the personality, an analysis, is undertaken, only a certain number of complexes, varying with the individual, can be made conscious. The rest continue to exist

[33] "Belief in Spirits," par. 594.
[34] On this point Freud and Jung agree.
[35] "Belief in Spirits," par. 591.

as "nodal points," as "nuclear elements," which belong to the eternal matrix of every human psyche, the collective unconscious, and Jung sees no reason why this residue "should not endure as long as humanity lasts,"[36] reaching out unceasingly into the domain of consciousness as a spontaneous manifestation of the unconscious. To his way of thinking, "primitive" means simply "primordial," and he attaches no value judgment to this qualification. Accordingly, "unmistakable traces [of complexes] can be found among all peoples and in all epochs . . . thus the Gilgamesh epic describes in masterly fashion the psychology of the power complex, and the Book of Tobit in the Old Testament gives the history of an erotic complex together with its cure."[37]

By way of illustration we might have recourse to a somewhat daring comparison and say: Although psychic energy operates continuously, it is "quantum-like" in nature. The quanta in our comparison are the complexes, innumerable little nodal points in an invisible network. In them, as distinguished from the "empty" spaces, the energy charge of the unconscious collective psyche is concentrated, acting, in a manner of speaking, as the center of a magnetic field.[38] If the charge of one (or more) of these "nodal points" becomes so powerful that it "magnetically" (acting as a "nuclear cell") attracts everything to itself (just as a cancer cell begins to proliferate, "devouring" the healthy cells and forming a state within the state) and so confronts the ego with an alien entity, a "splinter psyche" that has become "autonomous"—then

[36] "Complex Theory," par. 218.
[37] Ibid., par. 209.
[38] Frieda Fordham calls the complex a kind of "psychological magnet." (*An Introduction to Jung's Psychology*, 1953, p. 23.)

we have a complex. If a "nodal point" is enriched only by mythical or universal human material, we may speak of a complex originating in the realm of the collective unconscious; but if individually acquired material is *superimposed* on it, i.e., if it appears in the cloak of a personally conditioned conflict, then we may speak of a complex originating in the domain of the personal unconscious. Summing up, we may say that complexes have:

> *two kinds of roots* (they are based on infantile or actual events or conflicts)
>
> *two kinds of nature* (a complex may be "morbid" or "healthy")
>
> *two modes of expression* (a complex may, according to the circumstances, be regarded as negative or positive; complexes are "bipolar").

If we consider from how many different aspects every complex—according to Jung—can be viewed, it is easy to understand why, even in regard to this cardinal concept of depth psychology, so much confusion and misunderstanding were bound to arise among those who have not striven for a thorough understanding of Jung's ideas.

Complexes belong to the basic structure of the psyche

If we think them through, these views of Jung have vast implications. They imply that the complex actually constitutes the structure of the psyche, or in other words that the complex *in itself* is a healthy component of the psyche. Material deriving from the collective unconscious is never "pathological"; it can be pathological only if it comes from the personal unconscious, where it undergoes a specific transformation and coloration by being drawn into an area of individual conflict. When a complex is "divested" of the superimposed contents from the personal life of the individual, as occurs in the course of analysis when this repressed material of conflict is raised to consciousness, the true nucleus of the complex, the "nodal point" in the collective unconscious, is freed from all these contents in which it has been cloaked. The individual, who hitherto has been caught in his personal entanglements, is then confronted with a problem which no longer represents solely his personal conflict but gives expression to a conflict that it has been incumbent on man to suffer and solve from time immemorial. True release will never be achieved by too concretistic an explanation of the content of the complex, precisely because such an explanation always stops at the personalistically toned material that caused the disorder. Only an interpretation on the symbolic level can strip the nucleus of the complex from its pathological covering and free it from the impediment of its personalistic garb.

If a complex embedded in the material of the personal unconscious seems to stand in inexorable conflict with consciousness, its "nucleus," once laid bare, may prove to be a content of the collective unconscious. For example, the individual is no longer confronted with his own mother, but with the archetype of the "maternal"; no longer with the unique personal problem created by his own mother as a concrete reality, but with the universally human, impersonal problem of every man's dealings with the primordial maternal ground in himself.[39] Anyone

[39] Cf. the remarks on pp. 90-91 below concerning the problem of incest.

2 6

who has ever been through such a psychic experience knows what an immense relief this can be, how much more bearable, for example, it is for a son to conceive the son-father problem no longer on the plane of individual guilt—in relation, for example, to his own desire for his father's death, his aggressions and desires for revenge—but as a problem of deliverance from the father, i.e., from a dominant principle of consciousness, that is no longer adequate for the son: a problem that concerns all men and has been disclosed in the myths and fairy tales as the slaying of the reigning old king and the son's accession to his throne.

Accordingly, if a complex remains only a greater or lesser nodal point in the collective unconscious, if it is not swollen and overgrown by too much personal material, then it is not harmful but extremely fruitful, for it is the energy-giving cell from which all further psychic life flows; but if it is overcharged and becomes autonomous, or if it invades the realm of consciousness, it may take on any of the forms that generate neurosis and psychosis. And if the conscious mind cannot "cope" with these contents, the result, in peoples as well as in individuals, is the same: disorganization and disintegration. Thus it is solely the state of the conscious mind, the greater or lesser stability of the ego personality, that determines the role of the complex. Everything depends on whether the conscious mind is capable of understanding, assimilating, and integrating the complex, in order to ward off its harmful effects. If it does not succeed in this, the conscious mind falls a victim to the complex, and is in greater or lesser degree engulfed by it.

Neurosis and psychosis

Consequently the distinction between neurosis and psychosis—a distinction hitherto regarded as fundamental—can no longer be based on the content and energy value of the complexes in question, but solely on the "condition" of the individual's conscious mind. The fear of analysis, i.e., the fear that consciousness will be overpowered by complex contents, becomes all the more understandable, the more tensely and one-sidedly the individual clings to his habitual state of consciousness; for it is known that the danger of a loss of balance increases in proportion to the rigidity and one-sidedness of the conscious mind. The same is true of a consciousness which, in consequence of its lack of stability and consistency, must always fear inundation.

Neurosis lies on one side, psychosis on the other, of the dividing line drawn by the power of the ego consciousness to resist the break-through of unconscious contents. Often it is a question of merely a hair's breadth whether this resistance is broken only temporarily or permanently—theoretically both are possible in every lowering of the threshold of consciousness, every *abaissement du niveau mental* (Janet), whether it take the form of parapraxes, dreams, visions, fantasies, ecstasies, hallucinations, or is revealed in the material brought to light in the course of analysis. Complexes of the personal unconscious are less to be feared in this connection; the conscious mind can somehow deal with them. For the explosive dynamic of their "nucleus" is sufficiently insulated by the layer of personalistic, environment-conditioned experiences around it, which serve as a kind of buffer in its encounter with consciousness. Only when this "layer" is worn out, or when it is very thin to begin with (as is the case in many individuals threatened by psychosis), can the threat become really effective. For this reason the danger and the corresponding anxiety are greatest when the confrontation is with complexes of the collective unconscious, whose "explosive charge" can act as an earthquake shattering everything around it; and yet this danger can also open up the possibility of a total creative transformation and renewal of the psyche, and must for this reason be risked under certain circumstances. The difference between neurosis and psychosis thus becomes more fluid and the prognosis in principle more favorable.[40] The complex in its "seminal function" even deserves a place of honor as the life-renewing and life-promoting source whose function it is to raise the contents of the unconscious to consciousness and mobilize the formative powers of consciousness.

* *

The perspectives opened up by the Jungian view of the complex, as we have attempted to outline it here, are far-reaching and in a sense revolutionary. They developed organically, hand in hand with the general broadening and deepening of Jung's ideas; he himself has nowhere stated them in sharp and conclusive terms.

In order to gain a sound understanding of Jung's concept of the complex, we must never forget that this was

[40] Jung developed his views on this matter in detail in his paper "On the Psychogenesis of Schizophrenia" [C. W. 3] (lecture at the Royal Society of Medicine, London, April 4, 1939). Cf. Manfred Bleuler's excellent article, "Forschungen und Begriffswandlungen in der Schizophrenielehre 1941–1950" (1951). In summary Bleuler remarks here: "It seems as though the coming years would be devoted predominantly to the investigation of those older conceptions of schizophrenia, which regarded it wholly or chiefly as a personal disturbance in adaptation to the difficulties of life."

the revolutionary beginning which carried him beyond traditional psychology, paving the way for his fundamental discovery of the "dominants of the collective unconscious," or archetypes. In 1934, in his Eranos Lecture on the "Archetypes of the Collective Unconscious," he made the following significant statement: "The contents of the personal unconscious are chiefly the feeling-toned complexes, as they are called; they constitute the personal and private side of psychic life. The contents of the collective unconscious, on the other hand, are known as *archetypes*."[41]

With these words he pointed out an entirely new path which can no longer be ignored and the end of which is not in sight.[42] A kinship appears between the concepts of the complex and of the archetype; the relation between the two proves to be complementary and reciprocal. The notion of the complex—if it is to be fully understood—calls, spontaneously as it were, for an attempt to clarify the concept of the archetype.

[41] Now in C. W. 9, i: *The Archetypes and the Collective Unconscious*, par. 4.

[42] In 1912 Jung, in *Wandlungen und Symbole der Libido*, finally breaking with the purely concretistic view of the complexes as factors of the personal unconscious, recognized and investigated their archetypal content. Cf. p. 19, n. 25, above.

ARCHETYPE

Of the nature of the archetype

To expound the manifold and profound significance of the complex in Jung's psychology, without robbing it of its inner meaning, is itself an extremely delicate and difficult task, but any attempt to outline the concept of the archetype becomes truly a hazardous undertaking. It is impossible to give an exact definition of the archetype, and the best we can hope to do is to suggest its general implications by "talking around" it. For the archetype represents a profound riddle surpassing our rational comprehension: "An archetypal content expresses itself, first and foremost, in metaphors";[1] there is some part of its meaning that always remains unknown and defies formulation. Consequently a certain element of the "as if" must enter into any interpretation. No direct answer can be given to the questions of whence the archetype comes and whether or not it is acquired.

"Archetypes are, by definition, factors and motifs that arrange the psychic elements into certain images, characterized as archetypal, but in such a way that *they can be recognized only from the effects they produce.* They exist preconsciously, and presumably they form the structural dominants of the psyche in general. . . . As *a priori* conditioning factors they represent a special psychological instance of the biological 'pattern of behavior,' which gives all things their specific qualities. Just as the manifestations

[1] "The Psychology of the Child Archetype" (C. W. 9, i), par. 267.

of this biological ground plan may change in the course of development, so also can those of the archetype. Empirically considered, however, the archetype did not ever come into existence as a phenomenon of organic life, but entered into the picture with life itself."[2]

"Whether this psychic structure and its elements, the archetypes, ever 'originated' at all is a metaphysical question and therefore unanswerable."[3]

The origin of an archetype remains obscure, its nature unfathomable; for it dwells in that mysterious shadow realm, the collective unconscious, to which we shall never have direct access, and of whose existence and operation we can have only indirect knowledge, precisely through our encounter with the archetypes, i.e., their manifestations in the psyche. "You cannot," says Jung, "explain one archetype by another; that is, it is impossible to say where the archetype comes from, because there is no Archimedean point outside the *a priori* conditions it represents."[4]

However, the mere attempt to examine its phenomenology and describe it in this light represents an almost unprecedented attempt to gain an insight into the psyche of the archaic man who still lives within us, and whose ego, as in mythical times, is present only in germ, without fixed boundaries, and still wholly interwoven with the world and nature.

[2] "A Psychological Approach to the Dogma of the Trinity" (C. W. 11), par. 222. (Italics mine.—J.J.)

[3] "The Psychological Aspects of the Mother Archetype" (C. W. 9, i), par. 187.

[4] "Concerning the Archetypes, with Special Reference to the Anima Concept" (C. W. 9, i), par. 140, n. 27.

The historical development of the concept of the archetype in the work of Jung

Jung's manner of observing and describing psychological phenomena has always been undogmatic. With his extraordinary openness to new experience, he has always been willing to correct himself and develop. Accordingly, his concept of the archetype, formally as well as functionally, has undergone certain changes and developments, even though his fundamental picture has always remained the same. In 1917 he spoke for the first time of "dominants of the collective unconscious,"[5] by way of stressing the significance of those "nodal points," especially charged with energy, the totality of which constitutes the collective unconscious, and of bringing out their dominant functional character. Until then, from as early as 1912,[5a] he had used "primordial image" (*Urbild* or *urtümliches Bild*), a term inspired by Jakob Burckhardt.[5b]

By "primordial images" Jung then meant all the mythologems, all the legendary or fairy-tale motifs, etc., which concentrate universally human modes of behavior into images, or perceptible patterns. In the course of history these recurrent motifs have taken on innumerable forms, from the most remote conceptions of the primitives, down through the religious ideas of all nations and cultures, to the dreams, visions, and fantasies of modern individuals. Although there is some truth in the theory that such

[5] *Die Psychologie der unbewussten Prozesse,* p. 118 (cf. *Two Essays,* p. 65).
[5a] *Wandlungen und Symbole,* pp. 35, 142, 208, 245 (cf. *Symbols of Transformation,* pp. 32, 147, 216, 251).
[5b] *Briefe an Albert Brenner,* p. 6.

motifs have been disseminated by "migration," there are numerous cases where no communication was possible and "autochthonous" reappearance proves to be the only possible assumption.

The term "archetype," introduced in 1919[6] and today in general use, was taken by Jung from the *Corpus Hermeticum* (God is "the archetypal light") and from Dionysius the Areopagite: "That the seal is not entire and the same in all its impressions . . . is not due to the seal itself, . . . but the difference of the substances which share it makes the impressions of the one, entire, identical archetype to be different." "They say of God that he is . . . an Archetypal stone . . ." The term also occurs in Irenaeus: "The creator of the world did not fashion these things directly from himself, but copied them from archetypes outside himself."[6a]

In the form of latent possibilities as well as biological and historical factors, archetypal contents are a part of the psychic structure of the individual. The archetype corresponding to the individual's outward or inward life is actualized and in taking form appears before the camera of the conscious mind—is "represented" (Jung).

At first the notion of the archetype was applied by Jung primarily to psychic "motifs" that could be expressed in images. But in time it was extended to all sorts of patterns, configurations, happenings, etc., hence to dynamic processes as well as static representations. Ultimately it came to cover all psychic manifestations of a biological, psychobiological, or ideational character, provided they were more or less universal and typical.

For the sake of additional clarity, Jung drew a sharper

[6] See "Instinct and the Unconscious," par. 270.
[6a] *Hermetica*, ed. Scott, I, p. 140. / Dionysius, *On the Divine Names* (tr. C. E. Rolt), pp. 72, 62. / Irenaeus, *Adversus haereses*, II, 7, 5.

distinction between the terms "archetype," "primordial image," and "dominant," which at first he had used interchangeably. Particularly in his article "The Spirit of Psychology"[7] (1946) he insisted on the need for distinguishing between the "archetype as such [*an sich*]," that is, the nonperceptible, only potentially present archetype, and the perceptible, actualized, "represented" archetype. In other words, we must always distinguish sharply between the archetype and the archetypal representation or "archetypal image." As long as the archetype is an "invisible nodal point," still resting in the unconscious, it belongs not to the psychic but only to the "psychoid" realm.

"The archetype as such is a psychoid factor that belongs, as it were, to the invisible, ultraviolet end of the psychic spectrum. . . . One must constantly bear in mind that what we mean by 'archetype' is in itself irrepresentable, but that it has effects which enable us to visualize it, namely, the archetypal images."[8]

Only when it is expressed by individual psychic material and takes form does it become *psychic* and enter into the area of consciousness. Consequently, when we encounter the word archetype in any of Jung's writings, we shall do well to consider whether the reference is to the "archetype as such," still latent and nonperceptible, or to an already actualized archetype, expressed in conscious psychic material, an archetype that has become an "image."

Archetype, instinct, and brain structure

The archetype can be approached from many angles. Jung has given us an almost inexhaustible store of state-

[7] [Orig. in *EJ* 1946; tr. in *Spirit and Nature*. Revised in *Von den Wurzeln des Bewusstseins*; tr. in C. W. 8 as "On the Nature of the Psyche," to which version our references are made.]

[8] "On the Nature of the Psyche," par. 417.

ments on its diverse aspects. From these we can here single out only a few that throw light on certain of its essential characteristics.

". . . The unconscious, as the totality of all archetypes, is the deposit of all human experience right back to its remotest beginnings. Not, indeed, a dead deposit, a sort of abandoned rubbish heap, but a living system of re-actions and aptitudes that determine the individual's life in invisible ways—all the more effective because invisible. It is not just a gigantic historical prejudice, so to speak, an *a priori* historical condition; but it is also the source of the instincts, for the archetypes are simply the forms which the instincts assume."[9]

"Just as we have been compelled to postulate the concept of an instinct determining or regulating our conscious ac-tions, so, in order to account for the uniformity and regu-larity of our perceptions, we must have recourse to the cor-related concept of a factor determining the mode of appre-hension. It is this factor which I call the archetype or pri-mordial image. The primordial image might suitably be de-scribed as *the instinct's perception of itself,* or as the self-portrait of the instinct."[10]

". . . archetypes are not disseminated only by tradition, language, and migration, but . . . can rearise spontaneous-ly, at any time, at any place, and without any outside in-fluence. . . . This statement . . . means that there are present in every psyche forms which are unconscious but nonetheless active—living dispositions, ideas in the Pla-tonic sense, that preform and continually influence our thoughts and feelings and actions."[11]

[9] "The Structure of the Psyche," par. 339.
[10] "Instinct and the Unconscious," par. 277.
[11] "Psychological Aspects of the Mother Archetype," pars. 153f.

These statements by Jung raise the question as to how closely, in his view, the archetype is related to the "brain structure." Since there is much uncertainty in regard to this extremely subtle and important question, we shall cite a few more passages from the works of Jung:

". . . the archetype [is] a structural quality or condition peculiar to the psyche, which is somehow connected with the brain."[12]

"The archetypes are not whimsical inventions, but autonomous elements of the unconscious psyche which were there before any invention was thought of. They represent the unalterable structure of a psychic world whose 'reality' is attested by the determining effects it has upon the conscious mind."[13]

"Archetypes may be considered the fundamental elements of the conscious mind, hidden in the depths of the psyche. . . . They are systems of readiness for action, and at the same time *images and emotions*. They are inherited with the brain structure—indeed they are its psychic aspect."[14]

The archetype is not only an image in its own right but also "a dynamism which makes itself felt in the numinosity and fascinating power of the archetypal image. The realization and assimilation of instinct never take place . . . by absorption into the instinctual sphere, but only through integration of the image which signifies and at the same time evokes the instinct, although in a form quite different from the one we meet on the biological level. . . . It [instinct] has two aspects: . . . it is experienced as physiological

12 "Psychology and Religion," par. 165 (modified by R. M.).

13 "The Phenomenology of the Spirit in Fairytales" (C. W. 9, i), par. 451.

14 "Mind and Earth," in *Contributions*, p. 118 (modified). [C. W. 10.]

dynamism, while on the other hand its multitudinous forms enter into consciousness as images and groups of images, where they develop numinous effects which offer, or appear to offer, the strictest possible contrast to instinct physiologically regarded. . . . Psychologically . . . the arche-type as an image of instinct is a spiritual goal toward which the whole nature of man strives. . . ."[15]

"We are forced to assume, therefore, that the given brain structure does not owe its peculiar nature merely to the influence of surrounding conditions, but also and just as much to the peculiar and autonomous quality of living matter, i.e., to a law inherent in life itself. The given constitution of the organism, therefore, is on the one hand a product of outer conditions, while on the other it is determined by the intrinsic nature of living matter. Accordingly, the primordial image is related just as much to certain palpable, self-perpetuating and therefore con-tinually operative natural processes as it is to certain inner determinants of psychic life and of life in general."[16]

But in his most recent writings Jung has developed a vastly more far-reaching and indeed revolutionary view of this problem:

"If we are correct in this assumption, then we must ask ourselves whether there is some other nervous substrate in us, apart from the cerebrum, that can think and per-ceive, or whether the psychic processes that go on in us during the loss of consciousness are synchronistic phe-nomena, i.e., events which have no causal connection with organic processes. . . . Thus we are driven to the conclu-sion that a nervous substrate like the sympathetic system,

[15] "On the Nature of the Psyche," pars. 414f.
[16] *Psychological Types* (tr. H. G. Baynes), p. 557 (modified by R.F.C.H.).

which is absolutely different from the cerebrospinal system in point of origin and function, can evidently produce thoughts and perceptions just as easily as the latter. . . . During a coma the sympathetic system is not paralyzed and could therefore be considered as a possible carrier of psychic functions. If that is so, then one must ask whether the normal state of unconsciousness in sleep, and the potentially conscious dreams it contains, can be regarded in the same light—whether, in other words, dreams are produced not so much by the activity of the sleeping cortex, as by the unsleeping sympathetic system, and are therefore of a transcerebral nature."[17]

The biological aspect of the archetype

Insofar as the archetype has one aspect oriented "upward" toward the world of images and ideas, and another oriented "downward" toward the natural, biological processes—the instincts—it presents certain affinities with animal psychology.

"There is nothing to prevent us from assuming that certain archetypes exist even in animals, that they are grounded in the peculiarities of the living organism itself."[18]

Today this line of thinking has advanced to the point where Adolf Portmann, who has written a number of interesting works on the subject, speaks of the problem of

[17] "Synchronicity: An Acausal Connecting Principle" (C. W. 8), pars. 955, 957.
[18] *Two Essays on Analytical Psychology*, p. 69. In his article on animal psychology (in *Einführung in die neuere Psychologie*, 1931), K. C. Schneider speaks of a relation between object and subject, characterized by a form of action which "pre-exists potentially just as the body form of an organism is potentially pre-existent to its development."

"primordial images, preformed by heredity, in the experience of man and the animals,"[19] and observes: ". . . Biological research on the central nervous system of animals reveals structures which are ordered in the manner of *Gestalten* and can provoke actions typical of the species. . . ."[20] And he goes on to say: "Many people have forgotten how to experience consciously what is amazing in all living organization—consequently they are surprised

[19] In his excellent and extremely stimulating essay, "Das Problem der Urbilder in biologischer Sicht" (*EJ*, special vol., 1950, pp. 413 ff.), Portmann, on the basis of his biological experience, suggests a classification of the archetypal structures according to the following three stages, which would have their validity not only in the realm of animal life but also in that of human beings:

1. Structures determined by heredity, originating in extremely open formative dispositions and from the first possessing a strictly ordered *Gestalt* character, corresponding to the "releaser mechanisms" found in animals.

2. Structures . . . in which hereditary dispositions play only a very open, general role, but whose configuration is on the contrary determined by individual "imprinting," as has been recently established in the investigation of animal behavior. . . . Their particular character "is determined not by heredity but by imprinting."

3. Archetypal effects of a far more derived character than in the two preceding groups, or "psychic effects of secondary complexes, which originate in the ordered, formed, traditional heritage of a human group. Their genesis . . . leads through practice, habituation, and the reinforcing power of social evaluation and prestige, to complex structures which are formed secondarily in the unconscious and there attain to a permanent effect." Here "we are hardly justified in stressing the hereditary factor; on the contrary, it is the culture-conditioned factor that must be emphasized." And he concludes: "Whether the archetype is a deposit of innumerable experiences or whether it is not rather the *a priori* precondition for human experience, we do not know, and there precisely lies the question" (pp. 429 ff).

Jung's view would very well admit of this classification. Not, to be sure, in the form of three originally given, coexisting, and equivalent archetypal structures, but only as structures ordered in layers, so to speak, that is, formed historically, the second and third group merely constituting "envelopments" of the first. (Cf. also p. 55 below.)

[20] Ibid., p. 424.

40

that the quality of an animal's inward experience should be predetermined, ordered, and given by fixed structures."[21]

The building of the nest is just as much a process typical of the species as are the ritual dance of the bees, the defense mechanism of the octopus, or the unfolding of the peacock's tail. Here Portmann remarks: " . . . this ordering of the animal's inner life is controlled by the formative element whose operation human psychology finds in the world of the archetypes. The entire ritual of the higher animals has this archetypal imprint in the highest degree. It appears to the biologist as a marked organization of the instinctual life, which secures the supraindividual living-together of the members of a species, synchronizes the mood of partners, and hinders rivals from endangering the species by destroying one another in combat. Ritual behavior appears as a supraindividual order valuable for the preservation of the species."[22]

H. Hediger has attempted, in an important study, to show the action of archetypes in the instinctive behavior of the animals.[23] The supposedly free animal is not "free," but fitted into a space-time system within which its life is enacted in rigidly determined orders. If it is torn out of its familiar space-time system and artificially transplanted into a new "space," where it is not "at home," grave symptoms of uprootedness set in. The biological and social order compels the animal to remain in its home area if it is not to lose its viability. "The wonderful freedom of the animal," Hediger remarks, "is the projection of a human wish." This is true from the fish up to the most highly organized vertebrates. To this context belong the migra-

[21] Ibid., p. 422.
[22] Portmann, "Riten der Tiere," in *EJ* 1950, pp. 386 ff.
[23] "Bemerkungen zum Raum-Zeit-System der Tiere" (1946).

tions of the mammals, fishes, and birds, the millennial itineraries of certain wild animals, etc. The migrations of animals, the rhythms and rituals in man's daily life are correlates. Adherence to imprinted modes of behavior and experience is a safeguard, deviation from which must be paid for with anxiety and uncertainty. The animal will give up these "safeguards" only when constrained by outward force; man, through the relative freedom of his consciousness, has the possibility of departing from them voluntarily; thus he is exposed to the twofold danger of hybris and isolation. For in detaching himself from his original archetypal order, he cuts himself off from his specific historical roots.

In addition to Hediger and Portmann, K. Lorenz and F. Alverdes,[24] among others, have shown that the Jungian theory of archetypes might provide a suitable foundation for an overall view of human and animal psychology. Lorenz speaks of "innate schemata"[25] (that is, certain forms of "inborn reaction to characteristic stimulus situations"); these schemata are "independent of experience,"[26] and in them a "formal similarity to certain human relationships based on inborn schemata may be observed also in animal behavior."[27] He stresses that by this he does not

[24] Alverdes, "Die Wirksamkeit von Archetypen in den Instinkthandlungen der Tiere" (1939).

[25] A concept which he selected in 1935 in consideration of the important work of J. Uxküll, who as early as 1909 had pointed out, in his *Umwelt und Innenwelt der Tiere*, that every individual possessed a "world of connotation" (*Merkwelt*), through which it can "notice" certain situations; though, to be sure, he took this "world of connotation" to be a "structure of nerve configurations" situated in the brain.

[26] Lorenz, "Die angeborenen Formen möglicher Erfahrung" (1943), p. 283.

[27] Ibid., p. 291.

mean an "innate image" but only the "preformed potentiality" of such an image, and declares that it is "experience which fills the form with matter," and also that "certain types of human reaction cannot be explained by specific adaptation or expediency for the preservation of the race, but are direct manifestations of laws which attach to all living creatures as such . . . and which seem to be given *a priori*."[28] Although Lorenz did not fully appreciate Jung's theory of archetypes and disparaged it as a "generalization of special laws," it is not difficult to establish certain parallels. Also the modes of behavior which Alverdes designated as "archetype of the home," "archetype of the house," "mating archetype," "parenthood archetype," etc., are typical forms of experience in the animal as well as the human domain. They represent definite configurations of being and action and reaction, bearing a structural imprint in their "original pattern" but not in their individual manifestations.

"The term [archetype] is not meant to denote an inherited idea, but rather an inherited mode of psychic functioning, corresponding to the inborn way in which the chick emerges from the egg, the bird builds its nest, a certain kind of wasp stings the motor ganglion of the caterpillar, and eels find their way to the Bermudas. In other words, it is a 'pattern of behavior.' This aspect of the archetype is the biological one. . . . But the picture changes at once when looked at from the inside, that is, from within the realm of the subjective psyche. Here the archetype presents itself as numinous, that is, it appears as an *experience* of fundamental importance. Whenever it clothes itself in the appropriate symbols, which is not al-

---

[28] Ibid., p. 334. Cf. also Jung, *Two Essays*, p. 69.

ways the case, it puts the individual into a state of possessed-ness, the consequences of which may be incalculable."[29]

Here the biological, the psychological, and even in a certain sense the "metaphysical" planes lie close together. Hence Hediger's designation of the typical categories of animal behavior as "archetopes";[30] the term, being a psychological correlate of "biotope" (primary topographical unit[31]), is by no means farfetched.

Another field in which considerable work has been done on the problem of the preformed psychic structures, particularly in the last twenty years, is that of child psychology. Examples are the investigations of R. Spitz in collaboration with K. Wolf[32] and those of E. Kaila,[33] which have shown that, in the child from three to six months old, the social manifestation of the smile should be regarded as a response to the *Gestalt* action of the living human face, which "releases" innate archetypal reactions. The works of R. Kellogg[34] on the archetypal structure of the ego development of the child from two to four, as expressed in the child's scribblings and drawings, give us interesting clues.

"It is," Jung writes, ". . . a mistake to suppose that the psyche of the newborn child is a *tabula rasa* in the sense that there is absolutely nothing in it. Insofar as the child is born with a differentiated brain that is predetermined

[29] Jung, introduction to Esther Harding, *Woman's Mysteries* (1955), pp. ix f. [Tr. modified by R. F. C. H.]

[30] More recently Hediger has replaced this term by the broader concept of the "psychotope."

[31] This term was coined by Richard Hesse in his *Tiergeographie auf ökologischer Grundlage* (1924).

[32] Spitz, *The Smiling Response* (1946).

[33] Kaila, "Die Reaktionen des Säuglings auf das menschliche Gesicht" (1932).

[34] Cf. Jacobi, "Ich und Selbst in der Kinderzeichnung" (1953).

by heredity and therefore individualized, it meets sensory stimuli coming from outside not with *any* aptitudes, but with *specific* ones. . . . These aptitudes can be shown to be inherited instincts and preformed patterns, the latter being the *a priori* and formal conditions of apperception that are based on instinct."[35] "All those factors, therefore, that were essential to our near and remote ancestors will also be essential to us, for they are embedded in the inherited organic system."[36]

This is eminently confirmed by the observations carried out by the pediatrician F. Stirnimann[37] on newborn babies. For, according to Stirnimann, the psyche of the newborn babe is already structured when it comes into the world. "Anticipations," i.e., modes of behavior which belong to a later stage of development and appear prematurely, as it were, clearly disclose this structured character. "There is no postnatal psychogenesis," says Stirnimann, "only a development. . . . There is not only an inherited body structure, but also inherited instincts. . . . The psyche of the newborn child is like a photographic plate that was exposed in earlier generations; when it is developed, separate fragments of the picture appear here and there, until the whole picture is before us."[38] The view that all this springs from reflexes does not hold water. For though the archetypes, like the reflexes, act autonomously as it were, unlike the reflexes they have a meaningful character related to consciousness and are capable of manifesting themselves in all psychic as well as spiritual domains.

[35] "Concerning the Archetypes," par. 136.
[36] "Analytical Psychology and *Weltanschauung*" (C. W. 8), par. 717.
[37] *Psychologie des neugeborenen Kindes* (1940).
[38] Ibid., pp. 96-105.

While in the animal the physical and the psychic, this inherently inseparable pair, appear wholly fused and scarcely distinguishable,[39] in man the two domains soon present a possibility of observable parallelism and shortly thereafter of distinct "individuality." In Jung's opinion, "the original structural components of the psyche are of no less surprising a uniformity than those of the visible body. The archetypes are, so to speak, organs of the prerational psyche."[40] "For the archetype is an element of our psychic structure and thus a vital and necessary component in our psychic economy."[41]

"Just as the living body with its special characteristics is a system of functions for adapting to environmental conditions, so the psyche must exhibit organs or functional systems that correspond to regular physical events. By this I do not mean sense functions dependent on organs, but rather a sort of psychic parallel to regular physical occurrences."[42]

Realistic and symbolic understanding

From time immemorial, the daily course of the sun and the alternation of day and night have been expressed in a series of images—such as the myth of the dying and resurrected hero—and these images have been imprinted on the human psyche. Here we may speak of an "image analogy" to the physical process and assume that the psy-

[39] The instinct constitutes the "boundary stream" between the spheres of the physical and the psychic; one of its shores belongs to the land of the somatic, the other to the land of the psychic.

[40] "Psychological Commentary on the *Tibetan Book of the Dead*" (C. W. 11), par. 845, p. 518.

[41] "The Psychology of the Child Archetype" (C. W. 9, i), par. 271.

[42] "Structure of the Psyche," par. 326.

che has a structurally determined capacity for translating physical processes into archetypal forms or "images . . . which have hardly any recognizable connection with the objective process. . . . There is no ground at all for regarding the psyche as something secondary or as an epiphenomenon; on the contrary, there is every reason to regard it . . . as a factor *sui generis*."[43]

Man's need to understand the world and his experience in it symbolically as well as realistically may be noted early in the lives of many children.[44] The symbolic, imaginative view of the world is just as organic a part of the child's life as the view transmitted by the sense organs. It represents a natural and spontaneous striving which adds to man's biological bond a parallel and equivalent psychic bond, thus enriching life by another dimension—and it is eminently this dimension that makes man what he is. It is the root of all creative activity and is not fed by repressions (as psychoanalysis believed) but by the power of the initially imperceptible archetypes, working from out of the depths of the psyche and creating the realm of the spiritual. Thus, for example, the myth of the solar hero is the psyche's spontaneous "translation" of the sun's course and reflects man's growing awareness of the psychic processes accompanying the physical process. For "the archetype does not proceed from physical facts but describes how the psyche experiences the physical fact,"[45] i.e., the archetype makes it possible to translate physical factors into psychic factors. The word "translate" refers to that spontaneous activity of the psyche which we have hitherto been unable to account for in materialistic or biological

[43] "Concerning the Archetypes," par. 117.
[44] Jacobi, "Der Beitrag Jungs zur Psychologie des Kindes" (1950).
[45] "The Child Archetype," par. 260.

terms, and which bears witness to its ultimately spiritual and "immaterial" character.[46]

"The organism confronts light with a new structure, the eye, and the psyche confronts the natural process with a symbolical image, which apprehends the natural process just as the eye catches the light. And in the same way as the eye bears witness to the peculiar and independent creative activity of living matter, the primordial image is an expression of the unique and unconditioned creative power of the mind."[47]

Thus the archetype should be regarded first and foremost as the magnetic field and energy center underlying the transformation of the psychic processes into images. As long as it rests in the womb of the collective unconscious, it is only a "structure whose form is not at first determinable but which is endowed with the faculty of appearing in definite forms by way of projection."[48] The very etymology of the word "archetype" points to these characteristics. "The first element 'arche' signifies 'beginning, origin, cause, primal source and principle,' but it also signifies

[46] This is not affected by the view which postulates an analogy between the archetype and the historical and ethnic "mneme" of Semon's "engram theory." Even though Jung assumes that there are typical, fundamental forms of recurrent psychic experience—comparable to the "mnemic deposit"—and believes that these are grounded in the nature of life itself, so that theoretically they may be present even in the animal, still his concept of the archetype coincides only to a certain degree with the concept of "mneme." (Cf. *Two Essays*, p. 97, note.)

[47] *Psychological Types* (tr. Baynes), p. 557 (modified by R.F.C.H.).

[48] "Concerning the Archetypes," par. 142.

By *projection* we mean the unconscious, automatic extrapolation of a psychic content into an object, as an attribute of which it then appears to us. Everything that is unconscious in man is projected by him into an object situated outside his ego, so that the phenomenon of projection is a part of the natural life of the psyche, a part of human nature itself.

'position of a leader, supreme rule and government' (in other words a kind of 'dominant'); the second element 'type' means 'blow and what is produced by a blow, the imprint of a coin . . . form, image, copy, prototype, model, order, and norm,' . . . in the figurative, modern sense, 'pattern, underlying form, primordial form' (the form, for example 'underlying' a number of similar human, animal, or vegetable specimens)."[49] These concepts denote the process of "imprinting" through continually recurring typical experiences and at the same time refer to the "forces" and "tendencies" which lead empirically to a repetition of similar experiences and forms. They make it clear that "in the truly Protean realm of the psyche there is indeed a formative principle—dominant functions, or in other words 'archetypes'—and that in these regions we may speak of the action of an unformed and of a formative factor (*forma*) upon a formed element (*formatum*), and that this action takes place on different levels."[50]

Archetype and Platonic Idea

A certain relationship between the archetype and Plato's "Idea" is evident, but it is only partial, for the archetypes, as it were, "put the Platonic Ideas on an empirical basis."[51] Both signify something formed, "image-like," "seen," but the Ideas, unlike the archetypes, are "inherently immutable,"[52] and must hence be regarded as transcendent,

[49] Here we follow the excellent formulations of Paul Schmitt in his study "Archetypisches bei Augustin und Goethe," in *EJ*, special vol., 1945, pp. 98 ff.

[50] Ibid., p. 114.

[51] "Über den Archetypus" (1936), p. 264. [Passage not in C. W. version.]

[52] Schmitt, p. 99.

eternal forms existing *prior* to all experience. One is readily reminded of Jung's distinction between the "archetype as such" (not perceptible) and the "represented" or already perceptible archetype,[53] for the archetype in itself "transcends" the area of the psyche; it is beyond apprehension, "psychoid." Like the Platonic Idea it precedes all conscious experience. Here of course "transcendental" must be taken not as a metaphysical concept but empirically as signifying "beyond consciousness." If, on the other hand, the "Idea" appears within the categories of space and time in the realm of creation, i.e., in the realm of the conscious psyche, in the form of an "eidolon," then this eidolon, like the "perceptible archetype," combines a timeless factor (idea) and a temporal-material factor (mode of manifestation). In other words a bipolarity, an antinomy, is expressed. In this sense we may say with Jung that Plato's eternal Ideas, "stored up in a supracelestial place," are a philosophical expression of the psychological archetypes.[54] Over against the clarity of the Idea, the archetype has the advantage of dynamism. It is a "living organism, 'endowed with generative force.' "[55]

In the archetypes the psyche unceasingly supplies those figures and forms that make cognition possible. There is no important idea or view that is not grounded in primordial archetypal forms. They are primordial forms that arose at a time when the conscious mind did not yet think but only perceived, when thought was still essentially revelation; not invented but imposed on the mind from within, they are convincing by virtue of their immediacy.[56] Thus

[53] See p. 35, above.
[54] "On the Nature of the Psyche," par. 388.
[55] *Psychological Types* (tr. Baynes), p. 560 (modified by R.F.C.H.).
[56] "Archetypes of the Collective Unconscious" (C. W. 9, i), par. 69.

the archetypes are nothing other than typical forms of apprehension and perception, of experience and reaction, of active and passive behavior, images of life itself, "which takes pleasure in creating forms, in dissolving them, and in creating them anew with the old stamp: a process that takes place in the material, the psychic, and the spiritual realm as well."[57]

The archetypes are not inherited images

The often cited comparison of the archetype with the Platonic *eidos*, and the failure to distinguish between the nonperceptible "archetype as such" and the perceptible, "represented" archetype have caused the archetypes to be regarded, in a manner of speaking, as inherited "ready-made images." This has given rise to countless misunderstandings and unnecessary polemics.

It has been remarked in many quarters that from the standpoint of our present scientific knowledge acquired characters or memories cannot be inherited. Those who have raised this argument have assiduously overlooked the fact that Jung's archetypes are a structural condition of the psyche, which in a certain constellation (of an inward and outward nature) can bring forth certain "patterns" —and that this has nothing to do with the inheriting of definite images. They have refused to understand that these "primordial images," which are similar only in their underlying pattern, are based on a principle of form that has always been inherent in the psyche; they are "inherited" only in the sense that the structure of the psyche, as it is today, embodies a universally human heritage and bears within it the faculty of manifesting itself in definite and

[57] Schmitt, p. 99.

specific forms. Presumably a man living on another planet —if such men exist—would have a different psyche from ours, which would disclose an entirely different structure and entirely different primordial forms or archetypes.

For this reason it should be stressed that the archetypes are not inherited representations, but inherited *possibilities* of representation. "They appear only in the finished or shaped material as the regulative principles that shape it."[58] They are channels, predispositions, river-beds into which the water of life has dug deep. These "channels" form a kind of psychic mesh with "nodal points," corresponding, as we have seen, to the complex structure of the psyche, with its "nuclei of meaning." We must presume them to be the hidden organizers of representations; they are the "primordial pattern" underlying the *invisible order* of the unconscious psyche; down through the millennia their irresistible power has shaped and reshaped the eternal meaning of the contents that have fallen into the unconscious, and so kept them alive. They form a "potential axial system" and—like an invisible crystal lattice in a solution—are prefigured, as it were, in the unconscious. They possess no material existence; they are a sort of *éternels incréés* (Jung sometimes uses this Bergsonian term for them), which must first be endowed with solidity and clarity, clothed as it were by the conscious mind, before they can appear as "material reality," as an "image," and, in a manner of speaking, be "born." Even when we encounter them "within us" (in dreams, for example), the archetypes, as soon as we become consciously aware of them, partake of the concrete outside world, for from it they have drawn the matter in which they are "clothed." "The arche-

[58] "On the Relation of Analytical Psychology to the Poetic Art," in *Contributions*, p. 246 (modified). [C. W. 15.]

type is, so to speak, an 'eternal' presence," says Jung,[59] and to what extent it is perceived by the conscious mind depends only on the constellation[60] of the moment.

The "archetype as such" is an irrepresentable factor, a disposition which begins to operate in a given moment of the development of the human mind, arranging the material of consciousness into definite figures. "No archetype can be reduced to a simple formula. It is a vessel which we can never empty, and never fill. It has a potential existence only, and when it takes shape in matter it is no longer what it was. It persists throughout the ages and requires interpreting ever anew."[61] Its "fundamental pattern" is immutable, but its mode of manifestation is ever changing. This seems to set a definite limit to the possibility of interpreting and defining it. "Not for a moment," says Jung, "can we succumb to the illusion that an archetype can be finally explained and disposed of. Even the best attempts at explanation are only more or less successful translations into another metaphorical language."[62]

Archetype and Gestalt

Since the archetype is inherited "form," characterized at first by no specific contents, it is possible to make a connection between it and the so-called "*Gestalt* theory," by saying that what is "inherited" is precisely the *Gestalt*,

---

[59] *Psychology and Alchemy,* p. 211.

[60] In this context "constellation" means the state of consciousness to which the unconscious stands in a compensatory relation; it is manifested in the distribution of psychic energy and the corresponding charge of the archetype that has been touched and "called awake" by a current problem.

[61] "The Child Archetype," par. 301.

[62] Ibid., par. 271.

i.e., the psyche's ability to experience in *Gestalten* and to create *Gestalten* both in the literal sense and in the correct sense of totalities.[63]

The "*Gestalt* criteria,"[64] as formulated by Christian von Ehrenfels (1859–1932), founder of Gestalt psychology, also permit of certain analogies. These criteria are: a) the *Gestalten* comprise more than the mere sum of their elements; b) the *Gestalten* preserve their character and typical qualities even if their foundations are changed in certain ways. Thus they are "totalities" (like the archetypes), which cannot be defined but only "adumbrated" or experienced. "Totality signifies structure defined by meaning."[65] But as totalities they can be transposed and varied, and what remains unchangeable and recognizable is the invariant, the *Gestalt* as such.[66] A simple melody, for example, will always retain its fundamental form (*Gestalt*) regardless of the key it is played in, and anyone who is familiar with it can hear it even in the most complicated variations. A ground plan in the form of a cross may be surmounted by a church of any style whatsoever, whether Gothic, Moorish, baroque, or modern, without losing its underlying cruciform pattern. Similarly an archetype— for example, the archetype expressing the "creation of a

[63] See also Jacobi, *The Psychology of C. G. Jung* (London, 1951), p. 61; (New Haven, 1951), p. 58.

[64] A good summary of Gestalt psychology is provided by David Katz in his *Gestalt Psychology, Its Nature and Significance* (1951; orig. 1914).

[65] In this connection I refer the reader to the interesting and informative paper of K. W. Bash on "Gestalt, Symbol und Archetypus" (1946).

[66] Lorenz remarks (n. 26, above) that because the characteristics of "acquired memory images" are "not interchangeable in quality" they, unlike the "innate schemata," cannot be transposed. Certain analogies may be found between the idea of the "innate schemata" and Jung's theory of archetypes, and both show undeniable similarities to the Gestalt theory.

relationship" between two "realms"—may borrow its mode of manifestation from the most diverse spheres of reality and ideation and still retain its identity of meaning. In this case, bridge, rainbow, gate, mountain pass, compromise, connecting link can stand for the same meaning or at least fundamentally similar meanings, and yet, taken separately, each embodies a different aspect of it.

To the Gestalt psychologist, it is true, the *Gestalt* is a purely formal concept; it is largely lacking in the richness of meaning that is a constitutive element of the archetype. For although "meaning" in Gestalt psychology denotes "inner *Gestalt* order,"[67] it must be taken in a purely formal sense, like the "primordial pattern"; there is no connotation of content such as the archetype can express in the images aroused by its emotional charge. Still, "totality character" and "transponibility" are essential features both of the archetype and the *Gestalt*. "*Gestalten* are totalities, whose behavior is not determined by the behavior of their elements, but by the inner nature of the whole" (Wertheimer). And here again it should be stressed that neither the "favored *Gestalten*" (i.e., those possessed of pregnance) nor the archetypes are ready-made like the Platonic ideas; both result from the play of psychic forces, necessary consequences of the laws of order inherent in the psyche.[68]

The hierarchy of the archetypes

Every archetype is capable of infinite development and differentiation; like a robust tree it can put forth branches and thousands of magnificent blossoms. The question

[67] Katz, p. 83.
[68] Bash, p. 137.

of whether there are few or many primordial forms, or archetypes, seems to be futile. Ultimately they can be reduced to the possibilities of typical and basic experience, and conceivably to the unity of the primordial opposites— such as light-dark, heaven-earth, etc., the groundwork of creation itself.

The deeper the unconscious stratum from which the archetype stems, the scantier will be its basic design, but the more possibilities of development will be contained in it, and the richer it will be in meanings. An illustration is provided by the genealogies of the gods: "The essence of a god is unfolded in his descendants. The higher, i.e., earlier, the generative divine figures stand in the genealogical system, the greater is the number of beings contained in them, the richer and more varied are their meanings. And just as in a logical system the supreme concept remains qualitatively unchanged and quantitatively undiminished even after a number of subordinate concepts have been deduced from it, similarly the parent figures retained their unchanged plenitude of being and essence even after their particular modifications had been detached from them in the shape of their children."[69]

In the world of the archetypes we can accordingly establish a certain hierarchical order. We designate as "primary" those archetypes which are not susceptible of further reduction, which represent, as it were, the "first parents"; we term the next in line, their "children," "secondary," their "grandchildren" "tertiary," etc., until we arrive at those highly diversified archetypes which stand closest to the familiar domain of our consciousness and hence possess the least richness of meaning and numinosi-

[69] Paula Philippson, *Untersuchungen über den griechischen Mythos* (1944), p. 14.

tv or energy charge. Such a hierarchical chain might, for example, be formed of those archetypes which manifest the basic traits of the entire human family, of the feminine sex alone, of the white race, of Europeans, of Nordics, of the British, of the citizens of London, of the Brown family, etc. For it is incontestable that side by side with the archetypes which belong to the entire human race or the European, an inhabitant of London will embody others that are typical only of the dweller in London. The latter, however, must be regarded as variations of the former. The basic structure is laid down, but its individual spatiotemporal concretizations are imprinted by the time and environmental constellation in which they appear. As in the genealogies of the gods, these archetypes are "children" removed from the "primordial family," and accordingly they disclose the most diverse aspects. The primordial, essentially unchanging needs, the typical, eternally recurrent, basic experiences of mankind perpetuate the archetypes, and at the same time create those "magnetic tensions" within the psyche, which cause them to be manifested forever anew, in the most diverse variations and guises.[70]

Just as the formation of crystals rests on relatively simple principles, the archetypes, too, reveal certain basic features that assign them to definite groups.[71] "There are," writes Jung, "types of *situations* and types of *figures* that repeat themselves frequently and have a corresponding

[70] E. Schneider's idea of classifying the archetypes according to the threefold characteristics commonly assigned to the characterology of the person (namely, universal, i.e., collective; typical, i.e., pertaining to the group; and individual), seems to point in the same direction. See his article "Zur Psychologie des Unbewussten" (1952).

[71] Jung, "A Psychological Theory of Types," *Modern Man*, pp. 90ff. [C. W. 6.]

meaning. I therefore employ the term 'motif' to designate
these repetitions."[72] The typical motifs of the collective
unconscious are akin to the morphological and functional
similarities in the system of biology. "They are forms existing *a priori*, 'imprints,' or biological norms of psychic
activity."[73] But not only do the archetypes form the "primordial pattern" for personifications of partial aspects of
the psyche and hence for figures of all kinds; they can
also represent the "basic principle" for abstract relationships and laws.[74]

"The psychic manifestations of the spirit indicate at
once that they are of an archetypal nature—in other
words, the phenomenon we call spirit depends on the
existence of an autonomous primordial image which is
universally present in the preconscious makeup of the
human psyche."[75]

Even if we believe that a self-manifestation of the
spirit, an apparition of spirits, for example, is a mere hal-
lucination, it remains a spontaneous psychic occurrence
(not subject to our will). In any case it is an "autonomous
complex." The fact that the psyche of every individual, in
the course of his natural growth, develops into a totality
comprising such different components as the ego, the unconscious, the persona, the shadow, etc., is an archetypal
phenomenon. The crystallization of a more or less stable
ego, for example, is a development common to and charac-

[72] "The Psychological Aspects of the Kore" (C. W. 9, i), par. 309.
[73] Ibid., par. 309, n. 1.
[74] Cf. W. Pauli, "The Influence of Archetypal Ideas on the
Scientific Theories of Kepler" (in *The Interpretation of Nature and
the Psyche*), in which he cites Kepler's ideas on such matters as
the relation between Trinitarian conceptions and the three-dimen-
sionality of space.
[75] "The Phenomenology of the Spirit in Fairytales" (C. W. 9,
i), par. 396.

teristic of the human species. Like a seed the psyche bears within it the predisposition to full maturity, and realizes this predisposition in the form of archetypal processes. Thus individuation, man's potential development into a unique personality, is also an archetypal process, contained in germ in every psyche, whether it is actualized or not. And since all psychic life is absolutely grounded in archetypes, and since we can speak not only of archetypes, but equally well of archetypal situations, experiences, actions, feelings, insights, etc., any hidebound limitation of the concept would only detract from its richness of meaning and implication. Of course our intellectual judgment always seeks to define the archetype in unambiguous terms and so overlooks the essential, for its most characteristic feature, which we must above all bear in mind, is its ambivalence.[76]

On the collective unconscious

The collective unconscious as suprapersonal matrix, as the unlimited sum of fundamental psychic conditions accumulated over millions of years, is a realm of immeasurable breadth and depth. From the very beginning of its development it is the inner equivalent of Creation, an inner cosmos as infinite as the cosmos outside us. The widely accepted idea of the collective unconscious as a "stratum" situated *below* the conscious mind is therefore unfounded and misleading. This widespread tendency, particularly frequent among those trained in philosophy and theology, to identify the unconscious with something negative, unclean, or immoral, and hence to assign it to the

[76] "The Archetypes of the Collective Unconscious" (C. W. 9, i), pars. 8of.

lowest level of the psyche, stems from failure to distinguish between the personal and collective unconscious; in line with Freudian theory, the whole unconscious is taken as a mere "reservoir of repressions." But the collective unconscious is not made up of individual experience; it is an inner correspondence to the world as a whole. What is overlooked is that the collective unconscious is of an entirely different nature, comprising all the contents of the psychic experience of mankind, the most precious along with the most worthless, the most beautiful with the ugliest; and it is also overlooked that the collective unconscious is in every respect "neutral," that its contents acquire their value and position only through confrontation with consciousness.

This "neutral" character of the collective unconscious led Jung to designate it as "objective" in contrast to consciousness, which, unless taken in tow by unconscious currents, always adopts a personal standpoint guided by personal choice and attitude, and to coin for it the very appropriate term "objective-psychic." For out of it, through the archetypes, speaks the unfalsified voice of nature, beyond the judgment of the conscious mind and uninfluenced by the injunctions and prohibitions of the environment which leaves its deposit in the personal unconscious.[77] A topographical definition, distinguishing "up-

[77] A no less deplorable misunderstanding prevails in regard to the collective unconscious as the primal source of psychic energy, of the "undifferentiated libido," which is often confused with the similar-sounding Aristotelian concept of energy—hence a metaphysical concept. This perhaps is the point of departure for the erroneous but persistent objections raised by theologians to Jung's empirical observations regarding the idea of God in psychic life.

The attempt by E. Schneider (see p. 57, n. 70 above) to substitute an "instinctive unconscious" for the collective unconscious in order "to supply the archetypes with a tangible foundation" is doomed

per" and "lower" strata, might somehow be applicable to the "personal unconscious" as a receptacle of contents closely connected with instinctual life and repressed in the course of the individual biography. But in regard to the collective unconscious, we may be equally justified in representing it as over, around, under, or beside consciousness, insofar as this heuristic concept is susceptible of "representation" to begin with. "In my experience," Jung writes, "the conscious mind can only claim a relatively central position and must put up with the fact that the unconscious psyche transcends and as it were surrounds it on all sides. Unconscious contents connect it *backwards* with physiological states on the one hand and archetypal data on the other. But it is extended *forward* by intuitions

---

to failure precisely because the "archetypes per se," the sum of which makes up the collective unconscious, transcend consciousness and are therefore not "tangible." Their existence can be inferred only from the collective, universally human, transpersonal phenomenology of the psyche. As Schneider correctly says, their "formative action extends into the corporeal," and "reaching up into consciousness they are active in forming images." And it is true that "ordering factors" of the unconscious express themselves in the perceptible archetype. But the unconscious cannot be regarded merely as a "corporeal form-building and function-creating organ for the guidance of the body," because the archetypes also embody ideations lying beyond the realm of the corporeal, metaphysical facts and factors, symbols, etc., which are not included in the term "instinctive unconscious." Schneider expressly insists that his remarks on this should not be taken as "biological psychology," but his concept of the instinctive unconscious remains completely bound up with biology although he draws the conscious mind (and precisely because he draws *only* the conscious mind) into the picture and fails to consider the "intrusion" of the metaphysical into the psyche, and hence its function as a former of ideas. Jung designates the collective unconscious as "psychoid," i.e., transconscious. In terming it spiritual, instinctive, etc., one is making a statement about something concerning which, because it is unconscious, no statement can be made. One can only *describe the effects* that emanate from it.

which are conditioned partly by archetypes and partly by subliminal perceptions depending on the relativity of time and space in the unconscious."[78]

And even more specifically he writes: "We must . . . accustom ourselves to the thought that conscious and unconscious have no clear demarcations, the one beginning where the other leaves off. It is rather the case that the psyche is a conscious-unconscious whole."[79]

Archetype and synchronicity

The phenomena, sometimes interpreted as "miracles" and sometimes as "pure chance," in which inner perceptions (forebodings, visions, dreams, etc.) show a meaningful simultaneity with outward experiences, regardless of whether they are situated in the present, past, or future— e.g., the phenomena designated as telepathy—[80] no longer belong wholly to this "middle region" of the conscious mind, but are all manifestations of that "border zone" in which the conscious and unconscious realms touch or overlap, as occurs when the threshold of consciousness is lowered and unconscious contents penetrate spontaneously into the area of consciousness. Thus, in a manner of speaking, they can be experienced and noted simultaneously, since the acausality and space-time relativity prevailing in the unconscious simultaneously enter and act upon the

[78] *Psychology and Alchemy*, p. 132.
[79] "On the Nature of the Psyche," par. 397.
[80] "As Rhine's ESP experiments show, any intense emotional interest or fascination is accompanied by phenomena which can only be explained by a psychic relativity of time, space, and causality. Since the archetypes usually have a certain numinosity, they can arouse just that fascination which is accompanied by synchronistic phenomena. These consist in the *meaningful coincidence* of two or more causally unrelated facts." *Aion*, par. 287, n. 1.

field of consciousness. What we have here is a linking of events which is not of a causal nature, but calls for a different principle of explanation.[81] Their ultimate causes are no doubt the archetypes.

The studies and investigations that Jung has long devoted to these phenomena have led him in the last few years to assume the existence of a novel principle of nature, which manifests itself under definite psychic conditions. "Space, time, and causality, the triad of classical physics," he writes, "would then be supplemented by the synchronicity factor and become a tetrad." In contradistinction to "synchronism" (simultaneity) he called this principle "synchronicity."[82] By this he wished to designate "a coincidence in time of two or more causally unrelated events which have a similar meaning"; this applies also to all "*a priori* factors" or "acts of creation in time."[83] "However incomprehensible it may appear, we are finally compelled to assume that there is in the unconscious something like an *a priori* knowledge or an 'immediacy' of events which lacks any causal basis,"[84] but which manifests itself wherever the constellation is suitable. In this connection Jung goes back to the old, never satisfactorily solved problem of psychophysical parallelism, examining it from a new point of view and attempting to give it new meaning.

Synchronicity, he writes, "possesses properties that may help to clear up the body-soul problem. Above all it is the fact of causeless order, or rather, of meaningful or-

[81] "Synchronicity," pars. 818f.
[82] Ibid., pars. 960f. "Synchronicity is not a philosophical view but an empirical concept which postulates an intellectually necessary principle."
[83] Ibid., pars. 965, 968.
[84] Ibid., par. 856.

deredness, that may throw light on psychophysical parallelism."[85] For physis and psyche may be regarded as
two aspects of the same thing, ordered according to a
meaningful parallelism; they are, as it were, "superimposed" the one on the other; they are "synchronous" and,
in their cooperation, not understandable on the basis of
causality alone. But this "acausal orderedness,"[86] as Jung
calls the unconscious factors, is nothing other than the
archetypal structure of the collective unconscious; the
archetype, when it becomes perceptible to the conscious
mind, "is *the introspectively recognizable form of a priori
psychic orderedness.*"[87] By its increased energy charge or
numinous effect it evokes the intensified emotionality
that is the prerequisite for the emergence and experience
of synchronistic phenomena.[88] In this view, the archetype,
in addition to its function as a formative factor within the
individual psyche, takes on the broader significance of a
higher "order," to which "both the psyche of the individual and the object of perception are subordinated."[89] It
may be regarded as an *organizer of representations,* working from out of the unconscious, as a kind of "regulator
and organizing factor."[90] In comparison with our individual temporality, the life of the archetype is timeless and
unlimited.

[85] Ibid., par. 948.
[86] ". . . synchronicity in the narrower sense is only a particular
instance of general acausal orderedness—that, namely of the equiva-
lence of psychic and physical processes . . ." Ibid., par. 965.
[87] Ibid. (My italics.—J.J.)
[88] Ibid., par. 841.
[89] Pauli, "The Influence of Archetypal Ideas on the Scientific
Theories of Kepler," in *The Interpretation of Nature and the Psyche,*
pp. 151 ff.
[90] In Jung's view this characteristic is possessed in highest degree
by the archetype of the "psychic center," the self.

"Our life is indeed the same as it ever was. At all events, in our sense of the word it is not transitory; for the same physiological and psychological processes that have been man's for hundreds of thousands of years still endure, instilling into our inmost hearts this profound intuition of the 'eternal' continuity of the living. But the self, as an inclusive term that embraces our whole living organism, not only contains the deposit and totality of all past life, but is also a point of departure, the fertile soil from which all future life will spring. This premonition of futurity is as clearly impressed upon our innermost feelings as is the historical aspect. The idea of immortality follows legitimately from these psychological premises."[91]

Thus the archetype, like everything that is psychologically alive, has the essential attribute of *bipolarity*. Like a Janus head, it is turned both "forwards" and "backwards," integrating into a meaningful whole all the possibilities of that which has been and of that which is still to come. On the basis of this bipolarity its "healing" aspect may be viewed as a fragment of anticipatory psychological development and utilized in psychotherapy.

"Just as all archetypes have a positive, favorable, bright side that points upwards, so also they have one that points downwards, partly negative and unfavorable, partly chthonic. . . ."[92] "In the unconscious the individual archetypes are not insulated from one another, but are in a state of contamination, of complete mutual interpenetration and

[91] *Two Essays*, p. 190. Modern biology has attempted to explain it on the basis of the "eternal life" of the original cell.

[92] "The Spirit in Fairytales," par. 413. In discussing the complexes we have already seen that a contradictory, contrapuntal structure is an essential characteristic of the psyche, which makes it fundamentally impossible to apprehend it fully on a purely rational basis.

fusion."[93] Often it is "a well-nigh hopeless undertaking to tear a single archetype out of the living tissue of the psyche; but despite their interwovenness they do form units of meaning that can be apprehended intuitively."[94]

Archetype and consciousness

"The changes that may befall a man are not infinitely variable; they are variations of certain typical occurrences which are limited in number. When therefore a distressing situation arises, the corresponding archetype will be constellated in the unconscious. Since this archetype is numinous, i.e., possesses a specific energy, it will attract to itself the contents of consciousness—conscious ideas that render it perceptible and hence capable of conscious realization. Its passing over into consciousness is felt as an illumination, a revelation, or a 'saving idea.' "[95]

Only when the archetypes come into contact with the conscious mind, that is, when the light of consciousness falls on them and their contours begin to emerge from the darkness and to fill with individual content, can the conscious mind differentiate them. Only then can consciousness apprehend, understand, elaborate, and assimilate them. "A psychic entity can be a conscious content, that is, it can be represented, only if it has the quality of an image and is thus *representable*."[96] Only then can it be assimilated in the course of analysis and translated into a conscious formula. This process is absolutely necessary, for the contents of the collective unconscious are precisely

[93] "Über die Archetypen des kollektiven Unbewussten," *EJ* 1934, p. 225. [This passage does not occur in the version in C. W. 9, i.]
[94] "The Child Archetype," par. 302.
[95] *Symbols of Transformation,* p. 294.
[96] "Spirit and Life" (C. W. 8), par. 608.

"energy-charged nuclei of meaning." They are often possessed of a magic and fascinating power and—like gods de-
manding to be propitiated—they must be divested of their
reality and autonomy by a "changing of names,"[97] i.e.,
translated into a communicable language, if they are to
fulfill their purpose in the psychic economy. Accordingly
Jung writes:

"Psychology therefore translates the archaic speech of
myth into a modern mythologem—not yet, of course, recognized as such—which constitutes one element of the
myth 'science.' This seemingly hopeless undertaking is a
living and lived myth, satisfying to persons of a corresponding temperament. . . ."[98]

If such a translation is successful, in analysis, for example, the instinctual energies present in the unconscious
contents are canalized into the conscious mind, where they
become a new source of energy.[99] A new bond is created
between our personal conscious world and the primordial
experience of mankind, and "the historical man in us
joins hands with the newborn, individual man,"[100] that
is to say, the locked gate to the roots and sources of
our psychic life is reopened. This accounts for the liberating effect that may result for a sick psyche, severed from
its natural order, when it encounters and comes to grips
with the archetypes.

When an individual finds himself in a grave and seemingly issueless psychic situation, archetypal dreams tend
to set in, indicating a possibility of progress that would
not otherwise have occurred to him. It is in general such

[97] "A Review of the Complex Theory," par. 206.
[98] "The Child Archetype," par. 302.
[99] "Belief in Spirits," par. 595.
[100] "Analytical Psychology and *Weltanschauung*" (C. W. 8), par.
695.

situations that regularly constellate the archetype, if not by dreams, then through encounters and experiences that stir up the unconscious. In such cases the psychotherapist, if he understands and knows how to make use of the language of the unconscious, is obliged to find a new solution to a problem that cannot be approached rationally. It is the patient's unconscious that steers him toward this solution. Once the patient is approached in this way, "the deeper layers of the unconscious, the primordial images, are activated and the transformation of the personality can get under way."[101] "The layman, having no opportunity to observe the behavior of autonomous complexes, is usually inclined, in conformity with the general trend, to trace the origin of psychic contents back to the environment. This expectation is certainly justified so far as the ideational contents of consciousness are concerned. In addition to these, however, there are irrational, affective reactions and impulses, emanating from the unconscious, which organize the material in an archetypal way. The more clearly the archetype is constellated, the more powerful will be its fascination, and the resultant psychological statements will formulate it accordingly as something 'daemonic' or 'divine'. . . . Such statements indicate possession by an archetype. The ideas underlying them are necessarily anthropomorphic and are thereby distinguished from the organizing archetype, which in itself is irrepresentable because unconscious. They prove, however, that an archetype has been activated. . . . It is very probable that the activation of an archetype depends on an alteration of the conscious situation, which requires a new form of compensation."[102] This compensation in

[101] "Synchronicity," par. 847.
[102] "The Dogma of the Trinity" (C. W. 11), par. 223 and n.

turn leads to a new distribution of psychic energy and a corresponding reordering of the psychic situation. In such cases, "we must follow nature as a guide, and what the doctor then does is less a question of treatment than of developing the creative possibilities latent in the patient himself."[103]

Often the archetype confronts the individual in the form of a seeming trifle, of something that scarcely attracts notice; and this is as true for the figures of the outside world as for those of the inner world. And yet, as Jung has aptly said, it has "fateful power. . . . The archetypes have this peculiarity in common with the atomic world, which is demonstrating before our eyes that the more deeply the investigator penetrates into the universe of micro-physics the more devastating are the explosive forces he finds enchained there. That the greatest effect comes from the smallest causes has become patently clear not only in physics but in the field of psychological research as well. How often in the critical moments of life everything hangs on what appears to be a mere nothing!"[104]

For this reason, according to Jung, "sooner or later nuclear physics and the psychology of the unconscious will draw closer together as both of them, independently of one another and from opposite directions, push forward into transcendental territory, the one with the concept of the atom, the other with that of the archetype."[105]

An example from the world of dreams

The following dream may serve as an illustration of the possible role and action of an archetype. It was dreamed

[103] *The Practice of Psychotherapy,* par. 82.
[104] "The Spirit in Fairytales" (C. W. 9, i), par. 408.
[105] *Aion,* par. 412.

by a French physician, an internist, thirty-five years of
age and very much a rationalist. This man's aptitude for
brilliant formulations, his intellectual vigor, had led him
to suppose that he was an outstanding physician and that
if his patients got well it was *his doing*; that an extraordinary power resided in his will. In this inflation of the ego,
he totally failed to see that the creative gifts which he had
possessed in high degree in his youth had been stifled and
that his emotional powers were also paralyzed and sick.
The unconscious strove, by means of a strikingly archetypal dream, to correct and compensate for this one-sidedness of his conscious mind, which was beginning to threat-
en his psychic balance. Here is the dream:

"*I am sitting on a stone bench in an underground cave
about the size of a room. Behind me and a little higher,
also sitting on a stone bench, there is a noble, priestly
figure (something like Sarastro in 'The Magic Flute') clad
in long white robes. He is sitting directly behind me, motionless; only his eyes show that he is alive. I am incon-
gruously wearing a tuxedo, a costume hardly appropriate
to the stone cave. The ceiling and walls of the cave are
covered with stones that sparkle like jewels. A girl is led
in. She is dressed poorly, in hospital style. She is in a
catatonic state and passively lets herself be seated on a
stone bench in front of me. She is absolutely inaccessible
and unreacting.*

"*Then I begin to speak with her. I speak to her gently,
kindly; I keep speaking to her, and slowly, gradually, her
stupor falls from her. She begins to move; she sits up and
finally begins to look at me with awakened, healthy eyes.
Before my eyes she is transformed from a psychotic into a
healthy young girl; the process of transformation continues*

*and she takes on fairy-tale qualities; in the end she dances
through the cave like an elf and disappears.*

"*All the while the high priest sat motionless behind
me on his raised chair, and I knew that it was he who
had cured the girl by his mana-influence. The dream left
me with a feeling of profound security and confidence in
the figure of this man. It was he who had the healing power that had passed through me.*"

A commentary on this dream is superfluous. It interprets itself. It is not the supposedly omniscient man, the
man of the will, who cures, but the power, "standing behind" him and "passing through" him, of the "archetype
of the spirit." If he humbly "lets it through," the hitherto
rigid and sick feminine-emotional aspect of the dreamer
is filled with new life, becomes once more healthy and
buoyant; his paralyzed poetic gift is restored.[106] Since the
hero (here the dreamer) is in a desperate situation and
for outward and inward reasons cannot accomplish a self-
cure, the necessary insight appears, compensating for his
deficiency, in the form of a personified idea,[107] the "Wise
Old Man," who brings help and counsel.

It would not be easy for anyone whose conscious mind
still possesses a spark of life, a vestige of receptivity, to
ignore the "message" of such a dream or to dismiss it
rationalistically as a "fantasy." It imposes itself on the
conscious mind, compels it to take notice, and so makes
possible a change of attitude. But if it should be rejected,
if the archetype speaking through it should not be recog-

[106] A detailed interpretation of all the elements and aspects of
this very meaningful dream does not seem necessary in the present
context.
[107] "The Spirit in Fairytales," pars. 401f.

nized, "then it appears from behind in its 'wrathful' form, as the dark 'son of chaos,' the evildoer, as Antichrist instead of Saviour—a fact which is all too clearly demonstrated by contemporary history."[108] And this is true not only of humanity but of all the individuals that comprise it. It is true of all those who, though manifesting the "best of good will," unwittingly draw themselves and everything around them into the menacing abysses of their unconscious: the many psychotics and neurotics who are convinced that the evil is never in themselves but only in others, who must therefore be persecuted and destroyed.

* *

"In reality we can never legitimately cut loose from our archetypal foundations unless we are prepared to pay the price of a neurosis, any more than we can rid ourselves of our body and its organs without committing suicide."[109]

For the archetypes, as the voice of the human species, are the great ordering factors, disregard or violation of which brings with it confusion and destruction. They may be regarded as the "unfailing causes of neurotic and even psychotic disorders, behaving exactly like neglected or maltreated physical organs or organic functional systems."[110] Emerging from the psychoid background, they have an *ordering* effect on the psychic process and also on the contents of consciousness, leading them by labyrinthine ways toward a possible totality, since they "determine the nature of the configurational process and the course it will follow, with seeming foreknowledge, or as though they were already in possession of the goal to be circumscribed by the center-

---

[108] "The Dogma of the Trinity," par. 178.
[109] "The Child Archetype," par. 267.
[110] Ibid., par. 266. Cf. also what has been said above on the relation between archetype and complex.

ing process."[111] Thus they are also the protectors and bringers of salvation which can overcome every blockage and effectively and meaningfully bridge any split. He who speaks with the "primordial images" speaks "with a thousand voices; he enthralls and overpowers, while at the same time he lifts the idea he is trying to express out of the occasional and the transitory into the realm of the ever-enduring. He transmutes our personal destiny into the destiny of mankind, thereby evoking in us all those beneficent forces that ever and anon have enabled mankind to find a refuge from every peril and to outlive the longest night."[112]

[111] "On the Nature of the Psyche," par. 495.
[112] "On the Relation of Analytical Psychology to the Poetic Art," in *Contributions*, p. 248. [C. W. 15; here tr. R.F.C.H.]

SYMBOL

Archetype and symbol

When the archetype manifests itself in the here and now
of space and time, it can be perceived in some form by
the conscious mind. Then we speak of a *symbol*. This
means that every symbol is at the same time an archetype,
that it is determined by a nonperceptible "archetype *per
se*." In order to appear as a symbol it must, in other words,
have "an archetypal ground plan." But an archetype
is not necessarily identical with a symbol. As a structure
of indefinable content, as a "system of readiness," "an
invisible center of energy," etc. (we have previously characterized the "archetype as such" in these terms), it is, nevertheless, always a potential symbol, and whenever a general
psychic constellation, a suitable situation of consciousness,
is present, its "dynamic nucleus" is *ready to actualize itself and manifest itself as a symbol.*

The psyche "is, in fact, the only immediate experience
we can have and the *sine qua non* of the subjective reality
of the world. The symbols it creates are always grounded
in the unconscious archetype, but their manifest forms
are moulded by the ideas acquired by the conscious mind.
The archetypes are the numinous, structural elements of
the psyche and possess a certain autonomy and specific
energy which enables them to attract, out of the conscious
mind, those contents which are best suited to themselves."[1] "The unconscious provides, as it were, the arche-

[1] *Symbols of Transformation*, p. 232.

typal form, which in itself is empty and therefore irrepresentable. But, from the conscious side, it is immediately
filled out with the representational material that is akin to
it or similar to it, and is made perceptible."[2]

For as soon as the collective human core of the archetype, which represents the raw material provided by the
collective unconscious, enters into relation with the conscious mind and its form-giving character, the archetype
takes on "body," "matter," "plastic form," etc.; it becomes representable, and only then does it become a
concrete *image*—an archetypal image, a symbol. To define
it from a functional point of view, we might say that the
archetype as such is concentrated psychic energy, but that
the symbol provides the mode of manifestation by which
the archetype becomes discernible. In this sense Jung de-
fines the symbol as the "essence *and* image of psychic energy." Consequently one can *never* encounter the "archetype
as such" *directly*, but *only indirectly*, when it is manifested
in the archetypal image, in a symbol, or in a complex or
symptom. As long as something is unconscious, no statement can be made about it; hence any statement about
the archetype is an "inference."[3]

[2] "Der philosophische Baum," in *Von den Wurzeln des Bewusstseins*, p. 491. ["The 'Arbor philosophica,'" C. W. 13, here tr.
R.F.C.H.]

[3] Unfortunately the belief that only what comes within the scope
of our sense organs is "real" and can form the foundation of a
scientific statement is still predominant, even among numerous
psychiatrists and psychotherapists. M. Boss, to whom depth psychology is indebted for many valuable contributions, shows in his
book *Der Traum und seine Auslegung* (1953), especially in the
chapter on the archetype, that he takes this standpoint. He cannot
accept concepts such as archetype, symbol, or the unconscious in
general, for that matter, even as working hypotheses. For him they
represent empty, meaningless words. Consequently he reduces the
manifestations of the psyche to their behavioral aspect in relation

A good part of the confusion and misunderstanding stems from failure to bear this in mind—for here we have one of the essential differences between the two concepts, "archetype" and "symbol."[4]

A symbol is never entirely abstract, but always in some way "incarnated." For this reason even the most abstract relationships, situations, or ideas of archetypal nature are visualized by the psyche as specific forms, figures, images, objects, etc. (which may be concrete, as in the case of human, animal, or plant forms,[5] or abstract, as in the case of the circle, the cube, the cross, the sphere, etc.), or at least translated into events susceptible of being represented in images or pictorial sequences. It was this image-making power of the human psyche which, for example, cast the archetype of the "conflict between light and darkness, or good and evil" into the form of the hero's fight with the dragon (a primordial motif of many cosmogonies), or translated the archetype of the "idea of death and rebirth" into representable episodes in the life of a hero, or into the symbol of the labyrinth,[6] and in general created the boundless realm of myths, fairy tales, fables, epics, ballads, dramas, etc. We see this power at work in the great time-less creations of art, which perpetually link the primordial past with the distant future; we see it in the visions of the seers, in the apparitions and signs beheld by the

---

to the environment; psychic life is reduced to a system of potential relations to the world.

[4] In order to distinguish as sharply as possible between the archetype as such, the quiescent, non-actualized, and hence nonperceptible archetype, and the archetype which has already made its appearance in the area of consciousness, i.e., has been concretized by consciousness (transposed into an archetypal image, for example), the term "symbol" will be used throughout for the latter.

[5] "Der philosophische Baum," p. 379.

[6] See Karl Kerényi, *Labyrinth-Studien* (1943).

saints and religious seekers, in the fantasies of the poets, and last but not least in the nocturnal world of dreams, as from the inexhaustible treasure house of the archetypes of the collective unconscious it untiringly produces new and ever new symbols.

In speaking of such a translation of archetypal ideas into symbolic happenings—the Gospels provide magnificent examples of this—the terms "parable" or "metaphor" are sometimes used. But Jungian psychology prefers to use the word "symbol" for such sequences as well as for single, self-contained images. The fluid dividing lines, the often insurmountable difficulty of translating vision and experience into a conceptual language, and the continuous unfolding and deepening of Jung's insights account for the difficulty of discerning in his works the connections and differences between archetype and symbol that I have noted here. It cannot be stressed too often that we are trying to formulate and communicate in language phenomena which lend themselves only with difficulty to such treatment.

What is a symbol?

The word symbol (*symbolon*), derived from the Greek verb *symballo*, has long been the object of the most diverse definitions and interpretations. But all these definitions and interpretations are agreed that symbols present an objective, visible meaning behind which an invisible, profounder meaning is hidden. "Symbols," writes Doering, "are metaphors for the eternal in the forms of the transient; in them the two are 'thrown together,' fused into a unity of meaning."[7] And similarly Bachofen writes:

[7] Oskar Doering, *Christliche Symbole* (1933), p. 1.

"The symbol awakens intimations, speech can only explain. . . . The symbol strikes its roots in the most secret depths of the soul, language skims over the surface of the understanding like a soft breeze. . . . Only the symbol can combine the most disparate elements into a unitary impression. . . . Words make the infinite finite, symbols carry the mind beyond the finite world of becoming, into the realm of infinite being. They awaken intimations; they are tokens of the ineffable, and like it they are inexhaustible. . . ."[8] And in the same vein Creuzer: "In a sense, the symbol can make even the divine visible. . . . With irresistible power it draws the beholder to itself, and with the force of necessity, like the world spirit itself, it seizes upon our soul. In it moves the exuberant source of ideas; and what reason, aided by the understanding, strives to attain by a succession of inferences, it achieves through symbolism all at once. . . . We call the supreme manifestations of the formative faculty symbols . . . their characteristics are . . . instantaneity, wholeness, unfathomable origin, necessity. This one word signifies the manifestation of the divine and the transfiguration of the earthly image. . . ."[9] And Goethe: "Symbolism transforms the phenomenon into idea and the idea into image; in the image the idea remains infinitely effective and unattainable and even when expressed in all languages remains inexpressible."[10]

Symbols have acquired a permanent place in the language of Christian theology, as a designation for certain

[8] J. J. Bachofen, "Versuch über die Gräbersymbolik der Alten," in *Mutterrecht und Urreligion* (Kröner edn., 1954), p. 52.

[9] F. Creuzer, *Symbolik und Mythologie der alten Völker*, I (1810), 63, 64.

[10] Goethe, *Maximen und Reflexionen*, No. 1113.

dogmatic contents and religious processes.[11] But there is hardly a domain of cultural life, whether it be mythology, philosophy, art, technology, medicine, or psychology, where the word symbol has not been employed, and today it has almost become a cliché. Even so, there is still no modern, comprehensive work in which one may profitably seek its essence and meaning, or, above all, in which its profound psychological significance is investigated. Here again Jung has done pioneer work.[12] His researches give a compelling insight into the leading position of the symbol in the life of the psyche and hence in all cultural development.

Symbol and sign

Jung differentiates strictly between allegory, sign, and symbol. Here are some of his definitions:

[11] "The term symbol is used in a twofold sense: for the pictorial representation of religious ideas and for the authoritative ecclesiastical formulation of religious doctrines." (*The New Schaff-Herzog Encyclopedia of Religious Knowledge*, ed. Samuel Macaulay Jackson, XI, 199, s.v. "Symbolics.")

[12] Of the older major works, we might mention: F. Creuzer's work in six volumes, *Symbolik und Mythologie der alten Völker* (1810–23); G. H. von Schubert, *Die Symbolik des Traumes* (1840); C. G. Carus, *Symbolik der menschlichen Gestalt* (1853), a work that is still fascinating; J. J. Bachofen, *Versuch über die Gräbersymbolik der Alten* (1859); M. Schlesinger's fundamental *Geschichte des Symbols* (1912; Supplement, 1930); and Ernst Cassirer's *Philosophie der symbolischen Formen* (3 vols.; 1923–1929; tr., *The Philosophy of Symbolic Forms*, 1953-57). With his *Problems of Mysticism and Its Symbolism* (1915; orig. in German, 1914), Herbert Silberer has provided a kind of bridge to the Jungian conceptions. And among more recent writers: Jean Piaget, *Play, Dreams and Imitation in Childhood* (1951; orig. in French, 1945), a careful and impressive investigation of symbol formation in the child; Erich Fromm, *The Forgotten Language* (1952), a not very original, neo-Freudian attempt to explain the language of dreams; and finally,

"Every view which interprets the symbolic expression as an analogue or an abbreviated designation for a known thing is *semiotic*. A view which interprets the symbolic expression as the best possible formulation of a relatively unknown thing which cannot for that reason be more clearly or characteristically represented is *symbolic*. A view which interprets the symbolic expression as an intentional paraphrase or transmogrification of a known thing is *allegoric*."[13] "An expression that stands for a known thing always remains a mere sign and is never a symbol. It is, therefore, quite impossible to create a living symbol, i.e., one that is pregnant with meaning, from known associations."[14]

Basically signs and symbols belong to two different planes of reality. Cassirer puts it very aptly: "A signal is a part of the physical world of *being*; a symbol is a part of the human world of *meaning*."[15] Rather than as an

---

W. M. Urban, *Language and Reality: the Philosophy and Principles of Symbolism* (1939), an extremely well-written work, which embodies a number of Jung's observations and formulations.

[13] *Psychological Types* (tr. Baynes), p. 601 (modified).

"Symbol" is defined as follows in Meyer's *Konversationslexikon*, I, 371: "Whereas a symbol is a substitute and token for a mysterious edifice of ideas, an image for a vague and generalized psychic content, allegory consists in an animation of a clearly known concept or in an image employed to cloak a meaning accessible to the understanding and clearly definable (as, for example, the representation of justice by a female figure with sword and scales)." And in Howard C. Warren's *Dictionary of Psychology*: "An object, expression, or responsive activity which replaces and becomes a representative substitute for another."

In Creuzer's *Symbolik und Mythologie der alten Völker*, I, 70, we read: "The difference between symbolic and allegorical representation is that the latter signifies merely a universal concept, or an idea which is different from the representation; the former is the concretized, embodied idea itself."

[14] *Psychological Types*, p. 602 (modified).

[15] Cassirer, *An Essay on Man*, p. 32. (Italics mine.—J.J.)

"animal rationale," he suggests, man might be defined as an "animal symbolicum."

To this day a certain confusion prevails in the use of the terms symbol, allegory, and sign. Each author uses them from his own subjective point of view, often different from that of others. In most works on symbolism, the symbol is taken primarily as a "sign," a kind of abstraction, a freely chosen designation attached to the designated object by convention, as, for example, the verbal or mathematical signs. All sorts of subdivisions have been suggested in an endeavor to bring order into the confusion. Thus Jean Piaget makes a differentiation between "conscious symbols" (among which he designates symbolic drawings whose purpose it is to deceive the censorship) and "unconscious symbols" (whose content is unknown to the subject who makes use of them, as, for example, in dreams). But every symbol (still according to Piaget) may be designated in one aspect as "conscious" and in another as "unconscious"; every idea, even the most rational, conceals within itself unconscious elements, and every psychic process moves in an unbroken flow from unconscious to conscious and back again. In this Jung concurs.

Of the three sorts of symbols that Erich Fromm distinguishes in his book, namely, a) the conventional, b) the accidental, and c) the universal, only the last may be regarded as symbols in the Jungian sense. For here we have neither a "substitution" nor a "translation" of a content into another mode of expression: these symbols do not stand for something else, but themselves express or, one might say, represent their meaning. "It is not the case, however," writes Cassirer, "that the symbolic signs which we encounter in language, myth, and art first 'are' and then, beyond this 'being,' achieve a certain meaning; their being arises from their signification."[16] The more universal the stratum of the psyche from which such a symbol arises, the more forcefully the cosmos reveals itself in it. Take, for example, fire, water, earth, wood, or salt: when they are employed as symbols for a corresponding quality of immaterial, psychic reality, all the human experience that has ever been connected with their tangible materiality is expressed with inimitable simplicity and at the same time with a unique richness of meaning. The house may stand as symbol of the human personality; the blood as a symbol of life and passion; animals of all kinds as symbols for the various instincts and their stages of development in man, and so on. Indeed, as Jung says, perhaps even man himself is "an individual concretization, in space and time, of an eternal and primordial image —at least in [his] mental structure, which is imprinted upon the biological continuum."[17] And it was a mistake to call the theory according to which the inward state can be known through the outward sign a "signature" theory,[18] for the phenomena to which it referred were true symbols.

"Whether a thing is a symbol or not depends chiefly upon the attitude of the observing consciousness."[19] It depends on whether a man is able and in a position to regard a given object, a tree, for example, not merely in its

[16] Cassirer, The Philosophy of Symbolic Forms, I, 106.

[17] "The Phenomenology of the Spirit in Fairytales" (C. W. 9, i), par. 451.

[18] The idea of the "signature" was based on the doctrine of Paracelsus and other natural philosophers of the sixteenth and seventeenth centuries, according to which like can be cured by like, the form, color, etc. of a plant, for example, indicating what disease it will cure.

[19] Jung, Psychological Types, p. 603 (modified).

concrete manifestation as such, but also as an expression, a token for something unknown. Hence it is perfectly possible that for one man the same fact or object represents a symbol and for another only a sign.

"There are undoubtedly products," says Jung, "whose symbolical character does not depend merely upon the attitude of the observing consciousness, but manifests itself spontaneously in the symbolical effect it has upon the observer. Such products are so constituted that they would lack any kind of meaning were not a symbolical one conceded to them. Taken as a plain fact, a triangle with an eye enclosed in it is so meaningless that it is impossible for the observer to regard it as a merely accidental piece of foolery. Such a figure immediately conjures up a symbolical interpretation."[20]

Much, nevertheless, depends on the type of the observer, for there are individuals who always cling to what is concretely present, to facts, and others who put the accent on the hidden meaning of things, and so approach them with an attitude of openness to the symbol.

In Christianity, whose spiritual life is shot through with images and pictorial representations, the symbol is regarded as a sensuous sign for a suprasensory reality, but—as Weis points out—it is "never anything more than a mere sign, which symbolically and suggestively represents or communicates the transcendent reality, but does not contain, embrace, or substitute for it."[21] From this point of view all symbols are in themselves unreal, and the churches, particularly the Catholic Church, have always insisted that no symbolic interpretation must efface the fact of the

[20] Ibid., pp. 603 f. (modified).
The so-called "uniting (or unifying) symbols," the symbols of the self, belong largely to this category.
[21] A. Weis, "Christliche Symbolik" (unpub. lecture, 1952), p. 3.

reality of transcendence. But side by side with the doctrinal reality, which belongs to the metaphysical domain, stands the symbolic reality, which belongs to the psychological plane of experience, and what for one is only a sign is for the other a symbol, as Jung has demonstrated in a number of profound studies.[22]

"A knowledge of the universal archetypal background," Jung writes, "was, in itself, sufficient to give me the courage to treat 'that which is believed always, everywhere, by everybody' as a *psychological fact* which extends far beyond the confines of Christianity, and to approach it as an object of scientific study, as a *phenomenon* pure and simple, regardless of the 'metaphysical' significance that may have been attached to it."[23]

"Symbols are not allegories and not signs; they are images of contents which for the most part transcend consciousness. We have still to discover that such contents are real, that they are agents with which it is not only possible but absolutely necessary for us to come to terms."[24] "Although we naturally begin by *believing* in symbols, we can also *understand* them, and this is indeed the only viable way for those who have not been granted the charisma of faith."[25]

Symbols can, to be sure, "degenerate" into signs, but under certain circumstances, according to the context in which they stand or the attitude of the individual, signs can also be taken as symbols.

"Insofar as a symbol is a living thing," writes Jung, "it

[22] Among others: "A Psychological Approach to the Dogma of the Trinity" and "Transformation Symbolism in the Mass" (both in C. W. 11).
[23] "Dogma of the Trinity," par. 294.
[24] *Symbols of Transformation*, pp. 77 f.
[25] Ibid., p. 231 (modified).

is an expression for something that cannot be characterized in any other or better way. The symbol is alive only
so long as it is pregnant with meaning. But once its meaning has been born out of it, once that expression is found
which formulates the thing sought, expected, or divined
better than the hitherto accepted symbol, then the symbol
is *dead* . . . and it becomes a conventional sign. . . . It is,
therefore, quite impossible to create a living symbol, i.e.,
one that is pregnant with meaning, from known associations. For what is thus produced never contains more than
was put into it."[26]

Jung has given a particularly impressive example of the
different forms and meanings a symbol may assume in his
study of the "Philosophical Tree."[27]

The cross, the wheel, the star, etc., can be used to mark
stamps, flags, etc., and in this case they represent signs,
i.e., they indicate something; in another case, according
to the context and their meaning for the individual, they
can represent symbols. The cross, for example, may for
one man be merely an outward sign for Christianity, while
for another it evokes the story of the Passion in all its richness. In the former case Jung would speak of an "extinct
symbol," in the latter of a "living symbol," and say that
for one believer the Host in the Mass may still represent
a living symbol, while for another it has lost its meaning.
"Reflections about the symbolic character of a formulated
faith have proved, in many historical religions, to be the
first and decisive signs of their disintegration."[28] The
more conventional a man's mind and the more he holds to

[26] *Psychological Types,* p. 602 (modified).
[27] In *Von den Wurzeln des Bewusstseins.* ["The 'Arbor philosophica,' " C. W. 15.]
[28] Weis, "Christliche Symbolik," p. 6.

the letter, the more he will be barred from the symbol and the less able he will be to experience its meaning; he will cling to the sign alone and add his bit of confusion to the definition of the symbol.

It is not without interest, and throws light on the confusing changes in the interpretation of these concepts, to note how differently from Jung Goethe defined them in his Theory of Colors.

"Such an application [of the color], coinciding entirely with nature, might be called symbolical, since the colour would be employed in conformity with its effect, and could at once express its meaning. . . ."[29] "Another application is nearly allied to this; it might be called the allegorical application. In this there is more of accident and caprice, inasmuch as the meaning of the sign must first be communicated to us before we know what it is to signify, what idea, for instance, is attached to the green colour, which has been appropriated to hope?"[30] According to the Jungian view, both these forms would have to be designated as "allegorical" or "semiotic." On the other hand what Goethe calls the "mystical application" of color would be regarded by Jung as "symbolic." "Since every diagram in which the variety of colours may be represented points to those primordial relations which *belong both to nature and to human vision itself*, there can be no doubt that these may be made use of as a language, in cases where it is proposed to express similar primordial relations which do not present themselves to the senses in so powerful and varied a manner."[31] Here Goethe eloquently suggests

[29] *Goethe's Theory of Colours* (tr. C. L. Eastlake), par. 916, p. 350.
[30] Ibid., par. 917, p. 351.
[31] Ibid., par. 918, p. 351. (Italics mine.—J.J.)

the wealth of intimation, the meaning that can never fully be resolved, which characterize the symbol in the Jungian sense. And in the next paragraph Goethe continues: "When the distinction of yellow and blue is duly comprehended, and especially the augmentation into red, by means of which the opposite qualities tend toward each other and become united in a third; then, certainly, an especially mysterious interpretation will suggest itself, since a spiritual meaning may be connected with these facts; and when we find the two separate principles producing green on the one hand and red in their intenser state, we can hardly refrain from thinking in the first case of the earthly, in the last of the heavenly, generation of the Elohim."[32] Here we stand in amazement before the visionary power which could see the principle of totality concealed in the separation and convergence of antithetical color pairs as a symbol of the divine, and express it so profoundly. Anticipating future developments, Goethe even knew that it would be better "not to expose ourselves in conclusion to the suspicion of excessive enthusiasm; since, if our doctrine of colours finds favour, applications and allusions, allegorical, symbolical, and mystical, will not fail to be made, in conformity with the spirit of the age."[33]

The ability or inability, rooted in the psychic structure of the individual, to find access to symbols, is one of the reasons why Jung's method of deciphering dreams according to their symbolic content is so difficult for many to follow. For too many individuals are cut off from the figurative language of their psyche, and these are precisely the highly civilized, the intellectuals. They are no longer capable of grasping anything more than the outward

[32] Ibid., par. 919, p. 352.
[33] Ibid., par. 920, p. 352.

façade, the semiotic aspect of a symbol.[34] They have a secret fear of the ultimately inexplicable element that attaches to every authentic living symbol and thus makes a full rational understanding of it impossible. The "apodictic" character of the symbol can never do it full justice, for even its etymological significance, *symballein*, "to throw together," postulates a manifold, disparate content. As a uniter of opposites the symbol is a totality which can never be addressed only to one faculty in a man—his reason or intellect, for example—but always concerns our wholeness, touches and produces a resonance in all four of our functions at once. The symbol as "image" has the character of a summons and stimulates a man's whole being to a total reaction; his thought and feeling, his senses and his intuition participate in this reaction and it is not, as some mistakenly suppose, a single one of his functions that is actualized.[35]

The symbol in Freud and Jung

The divergence between the Freudian and Jungian conceptions of the symbol can easily be explained by their totally different theories of the unconscious. In the personal unconscious to which Freud confines himself, there are no archetypes, since its contents derive exclusively from

[34] Erich Fromm reports that under hypnosis persons having no knowledge of the interpretation of dreams were perfectly able to understand and interpret the symbolism of their dreams, but that on waking they showed no understanding of them at all and for the most part declared their dreams to be sheer nonsense. (*The Forgotten Language*, p. 19.)

[35] When Kant, for example, in his *Critique of Judgment* (par. 59, p. 222), speaks of a "wrong use of the word [symbol] subversive of its true meaning," he is assigning the symbol to a "mode" of intuition, hence taking it too one-sidedly.

the life history of the individual; hence these contents—
when they rise to the surface from repression—are at best
signs, "screen figures" standing for something that has already gone through the conscious mind. But when the contents of the collective unconscious—the archetypes—
emerge from the psychoid into the psychic realm, they must
be regarded as true symbols, because they stem from the
life history of the universe and not from that of the individual. For this reason also they *must exceed* the comprehension of the conscious mind, although they become
perceptible in a "garb" acquired by the assimilation of representational material and incontestably originating in the
outside world.

"Those conscious contents," writes Jung, "which give
us a clue, as it were, to the unconscious background are
incorrectly called symbols by Freud. They are not true
symbols, however, since according to his theory they have
merely the role of *signs* or *symptoms* of the subliminal
processes. The true symbol differs essentially from this, and
should be understood as the expression for an intuitive idea
that cannot yet be formulated in any other or better way.
When Plato, for instance, expresses the whole problem of
the theory of knowledge in his parable of the cave, or when
Christ expresses the idea of the Kingdom of Heaven in
parables, these are genuine and true symbols, namely, attempts to express something for which no verbal concept
yet exists."[36] The badge of the railway official, for example,
cannot be taken as a symbol of the railway, but merely
as a sign indicating that the man works for the railway.

Even though they are "condensed" and "overdetermined," the Freudian "symbols" are always causally ex-

[36] "On the Relation of Analytical Psychology to Poetic Art," in
Contributions, pp. 231 f. (slightly modified). [C. W. 15.]

plicable; in this sense they are unambiguous and unipolar. The symbol as Jung sees it is a psychic factor that cannot be analyzed or apprehended on the basis of causality, nor can it be determined in advance; it is ambiguous and bipolar. What we have said about Freud's and Jung's conceptions of the complex applies to their views of the symbol.

Here the difference between the personalistic-concrete and the symbolic-archetypal understanding and interpretation of symbols, the fundamental difference between Freud and Jung, becomes apparent. Let us take, for example, the much-discussed Freudian conception of the problem of incest. Jung does not deny that in some cases a child may desire sexual relations with his mother (or in the case of a girl child, with her father) or that such a desire, based on concrete experiences, may occasionally have brought with it all the psychic consequences observed and described by Freud and his school. But he is convinced that this understanding of the child's yearnings on the concrete, realistic plane alone is usually false and must lead one to false conclusions. For Jung the incestuous desires of children as well as adults should primarily be taken symbolically, as an expression of the universally human and forever recurrent yearning for return to the primordial, paradisaical state of unconsciousness, to a sheltered state free from responsibility and decisions, for which the womb is an unexcelled symbol. This regressive tendency, however, does not have a negative aspect only, but a very positive one as well; it implies the possibility of overcoming the personal bond with the real mother and transferring the psychic energy stored up in this bond to an archetypal content. At this stage the regressing libido tends to lose its sexual character and to express the incest problem in great archetypal metaphors typical of mankind, which touch the primordial ground of the maternal and at the same time point the way to a liberation from its seductive-devouring aspect, i.e., to a "rebirth." Even though the taboo that has been bound up with incest from time immemorial[37] bears witness to its enormous power of temptation, which can be combated only by strict prohibitions, it is undeniable that what on the biological plane would be regarded as a sinful deed may prove on a symbolic plane to be a meaningful and even necessary act.

Life proceeds on different planes—material, spiritual, biological, psychological, etc.—which may reflect each other in analogies. Above all, psychospiritual, immaterial being and happening can be embodied in images and symbols drawn from the perceptible, sensuous world. Certain psychic character traits may be symbolized by animals and their behavior, by objects, natural phenomena, and all sorts of things, and these in turn may find their correspondences in psychic qualities. For example, the sunrise represents a parallel to the awakening of consciousness, the night to a depressed mood, the bull to a blind impetuousness of psychic behavior. Ultimately everything in creation can become a symbol for the essential traits, qualities, and characteristics of man, while man represents parallels to the cosmos. Here we have the basis of the doctrine of the micro-macrocosm, which still has wide validity in the realm of the unconscious.

"We know," writes Jung, "that it is possible to interpret the fantasy-contents of the instincts either as *signs*, as self-portraits of the instincts, i.e., reductively; or as *symbols*, as the spiritual meaning of the natural instinct.

---

[37] With certain significant exceptions, as, for example, among the Hottentots, where the practice of incest serves as a proof that the mother has been surpassed or, in other words, that the man is no longer the mother's son.

In the former case the instinctive process is taken to be 'real' and in the latter 'unreal.' . . . Or is the incest . . . a regression of normal libido to the infantile level, from fear of an apparently impossible task in life? Or is all incest fantasy purely symbolical, and thus a reactivation of the incest archetype, which plays such an important part in the history of the mind?"[38]

Nor should we forget that while incest as union between the closest blood relations is a universal object of taboo, it is sometimes the royal prerogative (e.g., among the Pharaohs), and that in this sense, according to Jung, it symbolizes the union of the ego with the individual's own unconscious, the "other side"—a "blood relationship" within the psyche.

The ability to detach oneself from the carnal, the concretely real, to transpose it into the realm of the psychic, the symbolically real, which in consequence of its dual quality contains and expresses both realities—this characteristically human faculty points the way to the resolution and cure of crucial psychic disorders.

Or let us consider another problem which has taken on a particular urgency today, that of homosexuality. If it is taken not concretely but symbolically, one may discern in it a striving for union with an element of like sex, i.e., with the psychic aspect of oneself that has been experienced too little or not at all. Only then, fortified by this "increase" in his own sexual factor (whether male or female) does such an individual feel himself secure enough in his sex to be able to approach the opposite sex. Consequently his desire for a homosexual relationship is justified, but he misunderstands it by taking it in a biological

[38] "Psychology of the Transference," in *The Practice of Psychotherapy* (C. W. 16), pp. 175, 178 f.

and sexual, rather than a psychological and symbolic sense. To project it upon another individual, to experience it as a homosexual drive, is to misunderstand this desire and fail to see its profound meaning. Where this occurs, it can never come to a real fulfillment and can never, as it might with symbolic understanding, lead to an inner assimilation and resolution of the conflict.[39] Aside from the small percentage of individuals who may definitely be designated as homosexual in a physical sense, there are no doubt certain types who come into the world with a homosexual psychic structure and who therefore can be "cured" by no form of treatment, psychotherapeutic or other.

"There are processes," writes Jung, "which express no particular meaning, being in fact mere consequences, or symptoms; there are other processes which bear within them a hidden meaning, processes which have not merely arisen from something but which seek to become something, and are therefore symbols."[40]

Where we view something as causally conditioned, we do better to speak of a symptom rather than a symbol. Accordingly, says Jung, "Freud is justified, when, from his standpoint, he speaks of *symptomatic* rather than *symbolical* actions,[41] since for him these phenomena are not symbolic in the sense here defined, but are symptomatic signs of a definite and generally known underlying process. There are, of course, neurotics who regard their unconscious products, which are primarily morbid symptoms, as symbols of supreme importance. Generally, however,

[39] See also *Symbols of Transformation*, where Jung gives a richly documented example of the symbolic interpretation of the contents of the unconscious.
[40] *Psychological Types*, p. 606 (modified).
[41] Freud. Cf. *Psychopathology of Everyday Life*.

this is not the case. On the contrary, the neurotic of today is only too prone to regard a product that may actually be full of significance as a mere 'symptom.' "[42]

But whether the psychic products having a symbolic character that occur in neurotics should be set down as symptoms or as signs, or interpreted as symbols, can—as Jung tells us—be decided only by examining the individual case.[43] The explanation will vary with the type of case, the stage of treatment, and the patient's interpretive gift and maturity of judgment.

The symbol as mediator

Animals have signals and signs, but no symbols. Compared with the animal, man lives not only in a more comprehensive reality, but also in a new dimension of reality, namely, that of symbolism. In addition to the world of physical reality he has a world of symbolic reality, and he must give it expression if he wishes to rise from the animal world of instinctual drives to the creative being that he shares with the gods. All creation and even the smallest of its parts can become a symbol, an image con-

[42] *Psychological Types,* p. 606.

[43] An extremely interesting example of this may be found in Daniel P. Schreber, *Memoirs of My Nervous Illness.* In the course of his illness Schreber, a prominent German judge, built up a whole system of thought around his manias. He felt that he was being sexually persecuted by various male functionaries in the insane asylum who, he feared, would "use him as a woman" and eventually turn him into one. With the help of his "system" he was able to transform all his projections on concrete persons into symbolic relationships (e.g., the motif of "being used as a woman" into a betrothal with God the Father, his anxiety representations into divine spermata, i.e., inspirations, etc,). In this way he gave them a symbolic meaning, with which he was able to live and which inspired no fear. And this presumably accounts for his spontaneous cure.

veying meaning. The psyche as a mirror and expression of the outward and inward world creates symbols and transmits them from soul to soul. "For those who have the symbol the transition is easy," Jung quotes from an old alchemical treatise, meaning the "transition" between the psychic opposites, e.g., the unconscious and consciousness, obscurity and clarity, unfreedom and freedom, etc.[44]

What Jung means by the "bipolarity" of the symbol hinges on the above-mentioned twofold aspect of the archetype, pointing backwards and forwards, spaceless and timeless[44a]—and on its function of reconciling pairs of opposites, first and foremost that of the conscious and the unconscious, and hence also all the antithetical qualities that characterize them. This is indicated by the Greek root of the word, which suggests something that is "woven together, condensed, hence a 'characteristic,' an 'insigne' of a living entity";[45] but it is most aptly expressed by the German word for symbol, *Sinnbild*. The two words of which it is composed disclose the two spheres that the symbol combines into a whole: *Sinn* (sense, meaning), the integrating component of the cognitive and formative consciousness, and *Bild* (image), the content, the raw material of the creative, primordial womb of the collective unconscious, which takes on meaning and shape through its union with the first component. It is not difficult to discern a combination of masculine (form) and feminine (raw material) elements—for actually we have

[44] Cf. "Synchronicity," par. 930.

[44a] In proportion to the distance from consciousness, the categories of space and time become increasingly relative, until finally they dissolve entirely in the absolute unconscious and make room for a spacelessness and timelessness of events, where only the law of synchronicity holds sway.

[45] Schmitt, "Archetypisches," p. 110.

here a "coincidentia oppositorum"—and indeed the alchemists were extremely clear-sighted in referring to the symbol as a *"conjunctio,"* a "marriage." But the term applies only if this "marriage" is regarded as a perfect one, in which the two components are fused into an inseparable unity and wholeness and have become an authentic "hermaphroditus."[46] The soundness of this conception has been confirmed in innumerable fantasy and dream motifs, and in images and representations of all kinds, such as we find among mystics, alchemists, and painters, or such as are brought to the surface from the unconscious in the course of analytical work.

Discord in this "marriage," just as in the marriage of daily life, has bitter consequences. For as one of the "partners" wins superiority and the other is subjected, the symbol becomes predominantly a product of only one of the sides, and thus *more a symptom than a symbol*, namely "the symptom of a repressed antithesis."[47] And where there is complete disunion, it may be symptomatic of a corresponding dissociation between conscious and unconscious. At this moment it can be said that the symbol *is dead* ("extinct"). The two "halves" of the marriage have separated in enmity and withdrawn, each into its one-sided domain. The raw material of imagery, the content of the unconscious, lacks the formative power of the conscious mind, and consciousness dries up because the nourishing source of the image no longer reaches it. In terms of the psychological reality of the individual, this means

[46] For this reason the ultimate goal of the individuation process, psychic wholeness, is represented by the symbol of the hermaphroditic "filius philosophorum." Cf. *Psychology and Alchemy*, fig. 54, p. 109. Cf. also "The Psychology of the Transference," in *The Practice of Psychotherapy*.
[47] *Psychological Types*, p. 607.

one of two things: either the ineffable, mysterious, pre-
scient quality of the unconscious depths has vanished
from the symbol, so that its "meaning" can be fully known
and understood and it becomes a mere intellectual content, a mere "sign"; or else, cut off from the conscious
mind and from its power to assign meaning, the symbol
degenerates into a mere psychotic symptom. A symbol is
alive only as long as it is "pregnant with meaning," only
as long as the opposites, "form" and the "raw material of
imagery" (thesis and antithesis), combine in it to make
a whole (synthesis) so that its relation to the unconscious
remains effective and meaningful.

When we say it is "dead," we are referring only to the
perceptible, "represented" aspect of the archetype or symbol; its eternal "nucleus of meaning," its essence *per se*,
remains untouched. But it detaches itself, as it were, from
the psychic area, withdraws and maintains its "eternal
presence" in the realm of the psychoid, until a new constellation summons it to new life in a new guise, or rather to
a new manifestation, so that it re-establishes contact with
the conscious mind. Jung writes:

"A symbol that forcibly obtrudes its symbolical nature
need not be a living symbol. Its effect may be wholly re-
stricted, for instance, to the historical or philosophical
intellect. . . . A symbol really lives only when it is the
best and highest possible expression for something divined
but not yet known even to the observer. Under these
circumstances . . . it has a life-giving and stimulating effect."[48] "Inasmuch as every scientific theory contains a
hypothesis, and is therefore an anticipatory description
of a fact still essentially unknown, it is a symbol."[49]

[48] Ibid., p. 604 f. (modified).
[49] Ibid., p. 603.

Thus the symbol is a kind of mediator between the incompatibles of consciousness and the unconscious, between the hidden and the manifest.[50] "The symbol is neither abstract nor concrete, neither rational nor irrational, neither real nor unreal. It is always both."[51] It belongs to that "intermediate realm of subtle reality," which it alone can adequately express.

."The prospective meaning and pregnant significance of the symbol appeal just as strongly to thinking as to feeling, while its peculiar plastic imagery when shaped into sensuous form stimulates sensation just as much as intuition."[52] Its comprehensive wholeness provokes, as it were, the reaction of all four functions of consciousness.

This mediating, bridge-building quality of the symbol may be regarded as one of the most ingenious and significant devices of the psychic economy. For it constitutes the only truly natural and health-giving counterweight to the inherent dissociability of the psyche, which is a danger to its structural unity; it is the only factor that can combat this danger with any prospect of success. For in transcending the opposites by uniting them in itself (only to let them separate again afterwards, so that no rigidity, no standstill may ensue), the symbol maintains psychic life in a constant flux and carries it onward toward its destined goal. Tension and release—as an expression of the living movement of the psychic process—are enabled to alternate in a constant rhythm.

"What takes place between light and darkness, what unites the opposites, always has a share in both sides

---

[50] "Not every sign is a . . . 'mediator,' but only the sign in which a 'primordial gesture' becomes visible," says H. Kükelhaus (*Urzahl und Gebärde*, 1934, p. 58), fully in line with Jung.

[51] *Psychology and Alchemy*, pp. 270-71.

[52] *Psychological Types*, p. 607.

and can be judged just as well from the left as from the right, without our being any the wiser for it: all we do is to open up the opposition again. The only thing that helps us here is the symbol: in accordance with its paradoxical nature it represents the 'third thing,' which in logic does not exist—*tertium non datur!*—but which in reality is the living truth."[53] In this sense every true symbol is "beyond good and evil," i.e., it contains both meanings as potentialities, and the turn it will take for the individual depends solely on his state of consciousness and on the way in which the symbol is assimilated.

Jung calls this symbol-forming function of the psyche, i.e., its ability to synthesize pairs of opposites in a symbol, its *transcendent function.* By this he does not mean a basic function (such as the conscious functions of thinking, feeling, etc.), but a complex function composed of several factors, and by "transcendent" he implies no metaphysical quality, but the fact that this function creates a transition from one attitude to another.[54]

The symbol as a transformer of energy

"With the birth of the symbol, the regression of the libido into the unconscious ceases. Regression changes into progression, blockage gives way to flowing, and the pull of the primordial abyss is broken."[55]

[53] *Paracelsica*, pp. 134 f. ["Paracelsus as a Spiritual Phenomenon," C. W. 13, here tr. R.F.C.H.]

[54] An excellent symbol for the transcendent function is provided by the caduceus, the magic staff of the Greek god Hermes, with its interwined snakes. With this staff, Hermes, the mediator between the upper and lower worlds, put men to sleep and sent them dreams. (*Kleines Lexikon der Antike.*)

(For *transzendente Funktion,* I prefer the translation "transcending function," but here I follow the usage of the Collected Works.—J. J.)

[55] *Psychological Types*, p. 325 (modified).

For this reason Jung calls the symbol a psychic *trans-
former of energy* and points out that it has an eminently
"healing" character, that it helps to restore wholeness as
well as health. Here again we find a fundamental difference between the conceptions of Freud and Jung. In
Freud the "transformation of libido," sublimation, is "unipolar"; for in it unconscious, repressed material is always
canalized into a "culture-creating [i.e., positive] form."
In Jung the transformation of libido can be designated as
"bipolar," for it results from the continuous parting and
uniting of two conflicting elements; it is a synthesis of conscious and unconscious material.

The symbol, as a visible expression of the accumulated
energy charge of a "nucleus of meaning" within the psychoid collective unconscious, is able on the one hand to
relieve the tension and, on the other hand, through its
deeper meaning, to make a new impression on the psychic
process, i.e., to open up a new path and hence produce a
new concentration of energy. Thus, advancing from synthesis to synthesis, it unceasingly redistributes the libido[56]
and converts it into meaningful activity. This is what Jung
has in mind when he says that the words of Jesus to Nicodemus may be taken as a challenge, to mean: "Do not
think carnally, or you will be flesh, but think symbolically,
and then you will be spirit."[57]

How often a sense of release is produced when the
"carnality" disclosed in the crass naturalism of a dream
can be understood symbolically! Not, as one might suppose, because this enables the dreamer to evade his problems (sexual problems, for example), but because often it
is only such an understanding that can reveal the true

[56] By libido Jung, unlike Freud, means not sexual energy only,
but psychic energy in general.
[57] *Symbols of Transformation*, pp. 225-26. Cf. John 3:3-7.

meaning of the dream and bring help to the dreamer.

In Freud, for example, the little man who appears to the young woman in a dream and is immediately associated with "Rumpelstiltskin" stands for the phallus;[58] a Jungian would interpret him symbolically as a spirit goblin, a *kabeiros*, an archetypal figure whose alluring "help" brings ruin to woman, and threatens what is most precious to her but, precisely because she has recognized and named it, releases her from its power and leads her toward salvation. Both forms of interpretation may be simultaneously correct, but each opens up to the dreamer an entirely different realm of his inner reality. Or take the serpent. If it is interpreted "carnally," it too is a mere phallic sign; but according to Jung it is a libido symbol and may express psychic energy, power, dynamism, instinctual drive, etc., and ultimately the whole process of psychic transformation. Every kiss is a bodily kiss as well as an instance of psychic "fertility magic"; every cave is a womb and at the same time the site of a mystery, etc. The examples might be multiplied indefinitely.

This approach calls for an interpretation of dreams very different from the concretistic, personalistic interpretation. And indeed the Jungian method of interpreting dreams on the "subject level" has opened up entirely new aspects of understanding by showing their individual figures and motifs to be images of intrapsychic factors and conditions in the dreamer. This interpretation enables the dreamer to take back projections and solve problems within the area of his own psyche. Jung writes:

"I call every interpretation which equates the dream images with real objects *an interpretation on the object level*. In contrast to this is the interpretation which refers

[58] Freud, "The Occurrence in Dreams of Material from Fairy Tales" (1913), in *Collected Papers*, IV, 236 ff.

every part of the dream and all the actors in it back to
the dreamer himself. This I call *interpretation on the subject level*. Interpretation on the object level is analytic,
because it breaks down the dream content into complexes
of memory that refer to external situations. Interpretation
on the subject level is synthetic, because it detaches the
underlying complexes of memory from their external
causes, regards them as tendencies or components of the
subject, and reunites them with that subject."[59] Here, in
other words, the dream is regarded and treated as an "intrapsychic drama." This Jungian conception stands in
fundamental opposition to the approach of Freud, who
interprets dreams solely on the "object level." It is a
cornerstone of Jung's psychology and makes possible the
symbolic understanding of the contents of the unconscious. He attempted such an interpretation for the first
time in 1912 in his book on "Transformations and Symbols of the Libido,"[60] and his break with Freud was the
logical consequence of this development.

Of course Jung does not interpret every dream on the
subject level, but decides in each individual case which
level is appropriate.[61]

Interpretation on the subject level proves particularly

[59] *Two Essays*, p. 83. (For the terms *Objektstufe* and *Subjektstufe*,
I prefer the translations "object level" and "subject level," rather
than "objective level" and "subjective level" as adopted in the Collected Works. I have therefore modified this quotation accordingly.
—J.J.)

[60] *Wandlungen und Symbole der Libido*, renamed *Symbole der
Wandlung* (*Symbols of Transformation*).

[61] Where the dream deals with persons who stand in a vital relation to the dreamer, it is always interpreted on the object level
and, according to the individual case, sometimes on the subject
level as well, if this yields a satisfactory meaning; otherwise the
subject level is regularly applied. Strictly speaking, Jung designates
only the interpretation on the object level as analytic, in contrast to
the interpretation on the subject level, which he terms synthetic and
constructive.

fruitful when it is necessary to activate or revive the creative powers of the psyche, for the process in which the ego encounters and comes to terms with the symbols of the unconscious is extremely beneficial in removing and transforming the blockages and obstructions of psychic energy.

This process, which Jung (like Freud) calls a "transformation of energy from the (undifferentiated) biological form to the (differentiated) cultural form,"[62] "has been going on ever since the beginnings of humanity, and continues still."[63] Jung also believes that the deeper meaning of all mysteries and rites of initiation is of a symbolic nature and serves the purpose (unconscious, of course) of "transforming" the libido. From the standpoint of energy one may regard psychic processes as conflicts between blind instinct and freedom of choice or as a balancing of energy between instinct and spirit.

Individual and collective symbols

Not all archetypes or archetypal material are equally suited to the formation of symbols. Along with the many venerable symbols that the human spirit has formed in the course of the millennia, there are others which arise from the symbol-forming capacity of each individual psyche, but which are based on universal and fundamental archetypal forms and which, according to their expressive power and richness of content, have been taken over by mankind as a whole or by certain larger or smaller groups.

"The living symbol formulates an essential unconscious factor, and the more generally this factor prevails, the

[62] Cf. "On Psychic Energy" (C. W. 8), par. 113.
[63] Cf. ibid., par. 92.

more general is the effect of the symbol; for it touches the corresponding chord in every psyche."[64]

Many of these individual symbols are short-lived, limited to an individual or a few individuals. They help to clarify the ineffable, to throw bridges between obscure intimations and ideas that can be fully apprehended, so mitigating the isolation of the individual. But only when the universal archetypal pattern has shone through from behind the individual symbol and become accepted by the people as a whole, only when it has become a "collective symbol" in the manner of the innumerable symbols of mythology and religion with which we are familiar, can it fully exert its liberating and saving effect. An individual symbol, understood as a parallel to a universal symbol,[65] i.e., carried back to the "primordial pattern" common to them both, enables the individual psyche to preserve its unique form of expression and at the same time to merge it with the universally human, collective symbol.

Thus when a symbol emerges from the darkness of the psyche, it always has a certain character of illumination; often it may be charged with the full numinosity of the archetype that has become visible in it and act as a *fascinosum* which threatens to rend the individual apart unless he can integrate it with a collective symbol. How menacing and terrifying was the "face" that appeared to St. Niklaus von der Flüe in his vision,[65a] the face that he regarded as the face of God, and how many weeks of tormented strug-

[64] *Psychological Types*, p. 605 (modified).

[65] Cf. "Transformation Symbolism in the Mass" (C. W. 11).

[65a] To avoid any possible misunderstanding, I should like to make it clear that, in keeping with the whole tenor of this book, the visions of St. Niklaus von der Flüe are discussed only in their psychological aspect. The character of revelation accorded them by the Roman Catholic Church is not questioned in any way or even taken into consideration.

gle were needed before he could transform it into a collective symbol, namely, a vision of the collectively accepted Trinity, and so understand it! In the course of time every symbol undergoes a development of meaning, yet all the variations and stages of this development and unfolding disclose invariable, basic traits.

Symbols are never consciously devised; they arise spontaneously. They are not rational or a product of rational thinking or of the will, but rather result from "a psychic process of development, which expresses itself in symbols."[66] This is particularly evident in the case of religious symbols. They are not thought up; rather, they are "spontaneous products" of unconscious psychic activity; they have grown gradually in the course of the centuries; they have a "revelatory character."[67] And for this reason Jung writes:

"Experience shows that religions are in no sense conscious constructions but that they arise from the natural life of the unconscious psyche and somehow give adequate expression to it. This explains their universal distribution and their enormous influence on humanity throughout history, which would be incomprehensible if religious symbols were not at the very least truths of man's psychological nature."[68] And further: "Religions are psychotherapeutic systems in the truest sense of the word. . . . They express the whole range of the psychic problem in powerful images; they are the avowal and recognition of the soul, and at the same time the revelation of the soul's nature."[69]

If we consider the collective unconscious metaphorically

[66] Jung, Commentary on *The Secret of the Golden Flower*, p. 96.
[67] "The Soul and Death" (C. W. 8), par. 805.
[68] Ibid.
[69] "Zur gegenwärtigen Lage der Psychotherapie" (1934). ["The State of Psychotherapy Today," C. W. 10. Here tr. R.F.C.H.]

as the "universal soul" of human history, the universal as well as the individual aspects of this process of development may be found in any number of symbol sequences revealing parallel "patterns" (because they are based on the same archetypal pattern). In analytical treatment, therefore, according to Jung, every symbol should be considered in its collective as well as its individual context of meaning and as far as possible should be understood and interpreted on the basis of both.

Every human group, family, people, nation, etc., may produce the symbols it requires from out of its common unconscious. Individual and collective symbols are formed in outwardly different ways, but ultimately both are based on an identical structural pattern or archetype.[70] The points of contact between the individual religious symbols of numerous mystics and the official symbols of the various religions can be attributed to this common underlying pattern. The danger that this represents for the religions (i.e., the possibility of shattering their traditional forms) and the measures taken against it (excommunication, for example) acquire a broader meaning in this connection.

"Hence 'at bottom' the psyche is simply 'world.' . . . The more archaic and 'deeper,' that is the more *physiological*, the symbol is, the more collective and universal, the more 'material' it is. The more abstract, differentiated, and specific it is and the more its nature approximates to conscious uniqueness and individuality, the more it sloughs off its universal character. Having finally attained full consciousness, it runs the risk of becoming a mere *allegory*

[70] Cf. the "transformation symbolism" in the Catholic Mass, in nature, and in the mythologems and dreams of individual modern men, whose basic pattern is often strikingly similar.

which nowhere oversteps the bounds of conscious comprehension, and is then exposed to all sorts of attempts
at rationalistic and therefore inadequate explanation."[71]

The "archetype of the maternal," for example, is pregnant with all the aspects and variations in which "mother-
liness" can manifest itself, e.g., the sheltering cave, the
belly of the whale, the womb of the church, the helpful
fairy or the wicked witch, the ancestress, the Magna
Mater, or (on the level of individual life) one's own personal mother. Similarly "the father" is first of all an all-
embracing god-*image*,[72] the epitome of everything fatherly,
a dynamic principle which lives as a powerful archetype in
the soul of the child.[73]

Innumerable symbols are superimposed, as it were, on
the one archetypal "pattern." But the closer the stratum
from which they derive comes to our familiar objective and
concrete world, the more these symbols lose their symbolic
character. In the personal unconscious they take the form
of "screen figures," i.e., signs, and ultimately on the "highest" individual level they become the exact copy of a factual
and consciously intended content.[74] A similar thought is

[71] "The Psychology of the Child Archetype" (C. W. 9, i), par.
291.

[72] In order to avoid any misunderstandings on this score, it should
be stated expressly that this observation applies only to the "image"
of God as it appears in the psyche and has no bearing on His essence. As Théodore Bovet so aptly puts it in his *Die Ganzheit der
Person in der ärtzlichen Praxis* (1940), p. 116: "Science can never
encounter God; its conceptual system is adapted only to the shadows
cast by His light."

[73] "Mind and Earth," in *Contributions*, p. 124. [C. W. 10.]

[74] Cf. "Der philosophische Baum," in *Von den Wurzeln des
Bewusstseins*, p. 378: "The psychoid form underlying an archetypal
idea retains its character at all stages, though empirically it is capable
of endless variation. Even if the outward form of the Tree has
undergone many changes in the course of time, the richness and
life of a symbol express themselves more in its change of meaning."
[C. W. 13; here tr. R.F.C.H.] (Cf. p. 53 f., above.)

expressed by Goethe: "True symbolism occurs where the particular represents the more general, not as dream and shadow, but as living, momentary revelation of the unfathomable."[75]

The most impressive examples are provided by the mythologies of all peoples. The fairy tales and fables, whose basic motifs recur among most peoples, belong to a related category. Some are more primordial and naïve than the mythologems, others are more artfully and consciously elaborated. Jung also declares that the religious dogmas and symbols are empirically demonstrable correspondences to the archetypes of the collective unconscious and, from a psychological point of view, are based on them.[76]

"But, although our whole world of religious ideas consists of anthropomorphic images that could never stand up to rational criticism, we should never forget that they are based on numinous archetypes, i.e., on an emotional foundation which is unassailable by reason. We are dealing with psychic facts which logic can overlook but not eliminate."[77]

Jung, in his investigations, pointed to the Christian dogmas as "basic truths of the Church, which apprise us of the nature of intrapsychic experience in an almost inconceivably perfect way." All scientific theories are necessarily abstract and rational, "whereas dogma expresses an irrational whole by means of imagery."[78] It is something that has grown in the soul, not, as many sceptics suppose, something that has been worked out intellectually. Dogmas "are the repositories of the secrets of the soul, and this matchless knowledge is set forth in grand symbolical

[75] Goethe, *Maximen und Reflexionen*, No. 314.
[76] *Psychology and Alchemy*, p. 17.
[77] "Answer to Job" (C. W. 11), par. 556.
[78] "Psychology and Religion" (C. W. 11), par. 81.

images."[79] This accounts for their living and often astonishing effect on the souls of so many men.

But mythology, as a living reflection of world creation, is the form of manifestation, the "primordial guise" assumed by the archetypes in the process of becoming symbols. Since the basic forms of the archetypes are common to all nations and times, it should not surprise us to find amazing parallels in the myths that have arisen autochthonously in every corner of the earth. There is a primordial kinship between the great traditional mythologies with their mythologems and the archetypes with their symbols, which have condensed into "individual mythologies" in the individual human psyche. Who can say when the two first met? For the divine images of the great mythologies are nothing other than projected intrapsychic factors, nothing other than personified archetypal powers, in which human existence rises to the grandeur of the type and is concretized in its aspects. One of the profoundest students of these relationships, K. Kerényi, who has devoted several volumes to the problem, writes very aptly:

"In mythology the shaping is pictorial. A torrent of mythological pictures streams out. . . . Various developments of the same ground theme are possible side by side or in succession, just like the variations of a musical theme. For, although what 'streams out' always remains in itself pictorial, the comparison with music is still applicable, certainly with definite *works* of music, i.e., something objective, that has become an object with a voice of its own, that one does justice to not by interpretation and explanation but above all by letting it alone and allowing it to utter its own meaning."[80]

[79] "Psychology of the Transference" (C. W. 16), p. 193.
[80] Kerényi, "Prolegomena" to *Essays on a Science of Mythology*, p. 4.

Archetypes, mythologems, and music are woven from the same stuff, from the primordial archetypal material of the living world, and every future view of the world and of man will also emanate from this "matrix of life experience."

The ego between the collective consciousness and the collective unconscious

For a precise orientation in the world of the archetypes we must carefully distinguish the archetypes of the collective unconscious, which work upon the ego from the depths of the psyche and influence it in the direction of specific human behavior—both on the biological-instinctual and on the pictorial-spiritual level—from the archetypes of the *collective consciousness* as representatives of the typical norms, customs, and views prevailing in a particular environment. While the former, charged with magic and numinousness, lend meaningful form to the dynamism of the instinctual foundation of man and represent the spontaneous manifestation of his authentic, essential nature, the latter would seem to be pale copies of the unconscious archetypes. And yet when these pale copies cluster together, when a vast number of average opinions set themselves up as rules of psychic conduct, all sorts of mighty "isms" can arise. They seize power over man, and the measure of their power is the extent to which they alienate him from his instinctual foundation. Yet all "isms" have an archetypal foundation; for it is characteristic of the human species to fight the powers of the collective unconscious with those of the collective consciousness. For the most part the contents of the collective consciousness are not—and should not be—symbols. On the contrary, they are assumed to be purely rational concepts; but insofar as they have a history, they too rest on archetypal foundations, for which reason they inevitably contain a symbolic nucleus. Thus, for example, the absolute state consists of individuals deprived of all rights, ruled over by an absolute tyrant or an absolute oligarchy: an archaic social order of numinous nature recreated or repeated on a new plane.

Between the two great realms of the collective unconscious and the collective consciousness stands the ego, in danger of being swallowed up by both and able to preserve itself only by keeping a middle path between them.

". . . ego consciousness seems to be dependent on two factors: firstly, on the conditions of the collective, i.e., the social, consciousness, and secondly, on the archetypes, or dominants, of the collective unconscious. The latter fall phenomenologically into two categories. . . . The first includes the natural impulses, the second the dominants that emerge into consciousness as universal ideas. Between the contents of collective consciousness . . . and those of the collective unconscious there is so pronounced a contrast that the latter are rejected as totally irrational, not to say meaningless, and are most unjustifiably excluded from the scientific purview as though they did not exist."[81]

The ego loses its independence equally if it is sucked up by this collective consciousness or if it succumbs to the collective unconscious. The result in the first case is the mass man, in the latter the aloof individualist and crank or fanatic, again a victim of his drives.

When the content of a symbol is exhausted, when the

[81] "On the Nature of the Psyche," par. 423.

secret contained in it is either made entirely accessible to consciousness and rationalized; or when it has vanished from consciousness—i.e., has succumbed wholly to the unconscious, and the symbol has accordingly lost its archetypal opacity and numinosity—all that remains behind is the husk of the symbol, which then forms part of the collective consciousness. The contents of the collective consciousness are, one could say, empty shells of archetypes, simulacra of those of the collective unconscious, their *formal reflection*. Although they lack the numinosity of the archetypes, their action is *quasi-archetypal*, for their "ideals" are at first numinous—like the archetypes—but in time they are replaced by propaganda and pressure of opinion, which occasionally make use of authentic symbols, as in the case of the National Socialist swastika. From the relatively harmless "it is done" or "it is not done," pedantries that afflict young and old alike, to the intoxicating demagogic theories of paradise on earth which rob whole nations of their reason, one might list an endless series of rules, customs, laws, systems, and theories whose purpose it is to fetter man's natural dispositions from childhood on. Unlike the genuine symbol which touches and grips our whole being, the system, theory, doctrine, program, etc., merely befuddle and seduce our understanding without illuminating it. Thus many an intellectual succumbs to the slogans, the "isms," the collective commandments and prohibitions that come to him from outside, while he remains utterly uncomprehending toward the symbols that rise up from within him, for his mind has long since lost all relation to the other parts of his being.

Often we act and think—automatically, as it were—on the basis of concepts that we have taken over from the past or from our environment, according to typical prototypes and models. We repeat what has been handed down to us, what has been taught us and impressed upon us, what we have heard and read, and we suppose, because the process is so unreflecting and automatic, that all this has come out of ourselves, that it has been invented, found, thought by us, that it is our possession, because we can deal with it, handle it, so simply. Only when the collective consciousness and the collective unconscious come into conflict and make a battlefield of our psyche, do we become aware of how hard it is to free our personal individuality, the true core of our personality, from the clutches of these two powers. For this liberation requires an individual consciousness or ego which is able to differentiate, which has become aware of its limitations and thus knows that it must at all times retain its living bond with the two realms, the collective unconscious and the collective consciousness, if it wishes to maintain the wholeness of the psyche.

The symbols of the individuation process

Among the individual symbols special stress must be laid on those which characterize the process of individuation —a process of psychic development that aims at the broadening of the field of consciousness and a maturation of the personality. This process has been observed by Jung, and can be furthered by analytical work. Highly variegated symbols accompany the process and mark its stages like milestones. They are based on definite archetypes, which appear regularly in the material of the unconscious, e.g., in dreams, visions, fantasies, and which compel the individual to come to terms with them. The "guise" in which they appear as well as the time of their emergence are highly characteristic of the specific conscious situation of the individual. In connection with this situation, they take on a particular importance and enhanced effectiveness. The "guise," i.e., the mode of manifestation, can draw its material from all manner of sources, and hence it always depends on the individual and his situation whether a particular symbol is manifested as a positive or negative, as an attractive or repellent figure. But whatever form it may take, it will always possess the quality of a *fascinosum*. Among the symbols of the individuation process there are a few particularly significant ones, which appear in human or sometimes in subhuman or superhuman form, and which may be classified according to a series of types, "the chief of them being . . . the *shadow*, the *Wise Old Man*, the *child* (including the child hero), the *mother* ('Primordial Mother' and 'Earth Mother') as a supraordinate personality ('daemonic' because supraordinate), and her counterpart the *maiden*, and lastly the *anima* in man and the *animus* in woman,"[82] each of these representing a different sector of the psyche; and finally, the "uniting symbols," the symbols of the "psychic center," the self. As pictorial expressions of a supreme value, they are often represented by the figures of gods or

[82] "The Psychological Aspects of the Kore" (C. W. 9, i), par. 309. Cf. Jung's most important works, in which he records his experiences and thoughts in this connection. For example: "The Relations between the Ego and the Unconscious," in *Two Essays*, for the concepts of persona, animus/anima, mana-personalities; "The Phenomenology of the Spirit in Fairytales" (C. W. 9, i) for the Wise Old Man; Commentary on *The Secret of the Golden Flower* and "Psychology of the Transference" (C. W. 16) for animus / anima; *Aion* and *Mysterium Coniunctionis* for the symbolism of the self; *Symbols of Transformation* for the symbolism of the process of individuation; "Archetypes and the Collective Unconscious" (C. W. 9, i) for the concept of the archetype in general and in particular.

by symbols of the indestructible (stone, diamond, etc.), or they may also be of a purely abstract, geometrical kind, e.g., mandalas, which should be regarded as symbols of the basic order of the psyche as a whole.[83] But this does not mean that the symbolism of the self always takes the form of a mandala. Every created thing, big and little, lowly and sublime, can become a symbol of the self according to the state of the individual's consciousness. Of course a strict differentiation is not generally possible, for the similarity of such individual symbols to purely collective ones is often so baffling that only careful scrutiny can distinguish between them.

When consciously observed and guided, the individuation process represents a dialectical interaction between the contents of the unconscious and of consciousness; symbols provide the necessary bridges, linking and reconciling the often seemingly irreconcilable contradictions between the two "sides." Just as from the outset every seed contains the mature fruit as its hidden goal, so the human psyche, whether aware of it or not, resisting or unresisting, is oriented toward its "wholeness." Hence the way of individuation—though at first it may be no more than a "trace"—becomes deeply engraved in the course of the individual's life, and to deviate from it involves the danger of psychic disturbances. Consequently Jung says:

"The symbols that rise up out of the unconscious in dreams point rather to a confrontation of opposites, and

[83] "That numbers have an archetypal foundation is not, by the way, a conjecture of mine but of certain mathematicians, as we shall see in due course. Hence it is not such an audacious conclusion after all if we define number psychologically as an *archetype of order* which has become conscious. Remarkably enough, the psychic images of wholeness which are spontaneously produced by the unconscious, the symbols of the self in mandala form, also have a mathematical structure." ("Synchronicity," par. 870.)

the images of the goal represent their successful reconciliation. Something empirically demonstrable comes to our aid from the depths of our unconscious nature. It is the task of the conscious mind to understand these hints. If this does not happen, the process of individuation will nevertheless continue. The only difference is that we become its victims and are dragged along by fate toward that inescapable goal which we might have reached walking upright, if only we had taken the trouble and been patient enough to understand in time the meaning of the numina that cross our path."[84]

The psyche's capacity for symbol transformation

Side by side with the incessant *symbol-forming activity* of the psyche, which furthers its flow of energy or is impelled to illustrate it, we must also mention its *capacity to transform symbols*. The number of archetypes operative in man coincides with that of the "nodal points" of the collective unconscious and seems to be very great.[85] But the number of symbols based on them must be conceived as infinitely greater, since individual states of mind also play a part in their formation; their variations are indeed unlimited. "Their specific content appears only in the course of the individual's [or group's] life, when personal experience is taken up in precisely these forms"[86] (i.e., the archetypes). As our insights and experiences change, the meaning of a symbol can appear in an ever-changing light or open up to us gradually, so that this meaning and even

[84] "Answer to Job" (C. W. 11), p. 460 (modified).
[85] Cf. above, p. 24 and p. 55.
[86] Psychological Commentary on *The Tibetan Book of the Dead* (C. W. 11), par. 845.

the very form of the symbol are placed in continuously new
contexts and transformed accordingly.

The numinous, the mysterious, and the irrational have
been offered to us at all times, but recognized only by a
few. If the number of these few is steadily decreasing, it is
also because we seem to have lost the means of "offering"
the divine without "divulging" it. Every epoch has given
the mystery its own appropriate guise; but our era has not
yet found a suitable cloak for the numinous. It either lays
bare the secret or veils it beyond recognition. Jungian
psychology is one of the many attempts to find the new
"guise," the new language, and the new vantage point
that may help the present-day, rationally inclined man to
apprehend the irrational, and give him a feeling for it. It
helps him to satisfy his longing for the irrational—which
usually loses itself in errors and detours—by going back to
the eternal mediator between that which is accessible to
reason and that which is not accessible, namely, the symbol.[87]

Every myth must renew itself, just as the king in the
fairy tales must hand on his kingdom to his son as soon
as the son has accomplished the necessary deeds, i.e., as
soon as he has become ripe for it. At all times the myths
have had to be translated into the current psychological
language in order to find access to men's souls. Formerly,
for example, one spoke of the hero, the slaying of the dragon, etc.; today we say: personality, process of individuation, victory over the mother, etc. And just as the myth
always contained a mystery, so our present psychological
terminology is not merely rational. It is too much involved

[87] L. Szondi says: "We have three accesses to the unconscious.
In other words, the unconscious speaks three languages, the language
of symptoms, the language of symbols, and the language of choice."
(*Ichanalyse* [1956], p. 62.)

in our well-guarded inner life, too much compelled to express ideas that are only darkly surmised. Hence if we wish once more to experience myth as an unceasing activity of the depths of our unconscious, and understand it correctly, we must first translate it into our language, though when we do so it may often seem to us that we have lost its kernel and true meaning. But this is a false inference; on the contrary we have rescued the essence of the myth and integrated it with our world of ideas by the use of suitable terms. A vestige of mystery remains, however; it has not been possible, and it will never be possible, to translate this into abstract concepts, into a discursive language. The only appropriate expression for it remains the image, the symbol. Thus every man and every period give the symbols a new guise, and the "eternal truth" that the symbol communicates speaks to us in undying splendor.

The "metamorphosis of the gods" in our outward and inward worlds is inexhaustible and never ceases. Hence it can truly be said, "Every attempt at psychological explanation is, at bottom, the creation of a new myth. We merely translate one symbol into another symbol which is better suited to the existing constellation of our individual fate and that of humanity as a whole. Our science, too, is another of these figurative languages. Thus we simply create a new symbol for that same enigma which confronted all ages before us."[88]

Summary

The conclusions from what has been said thus far follow naturally.

"At the very bottom," in the primordial ground of the

[88] Cf. *Psychological Types*, p. 314.

psyche, are the *archetypes*, the "nodal points," i.e., energy-charged "nuclei of meaning" of the endlessly ramified and timeless psychic structure; they form the collective unconscious, the universal human foundation of *every* individual psyche. Here we must differentiate between the archetype as such, the nonperceptible archetype which belongs to the psychoid realm and which is present only as a structural factor and potentiality, and the archetype which has already become perceptible, or rather is "represented" to the conscious mind and for the most part should be conceived as a symbol. They are present *in the healthy and the sick alike* and are basically of the same nature in both. Just as buildings of different style and size may be erected according to the same ground plan, so the same basic archetypal pattern may serve as a foundation for the most varied structures. According to the content with which an archetype is filled, and according to the energy charge it obtains from that content, we can determine its "positional value" in the psyche's general frame of reference, its meaning, significance, and function.

An attempt to break down the course of its activity might reveal the following stages:

1. The archetype is quiescent, a structural factor in the psychoid realm of the collective unconscious, an invisible "nuclear element" and "potential carrier of meaning."

2. Through a suitable constellation—which may be conditioned by individual or collective factors—it receives additional energy; its charge is increased, and its dynamic operation begins. The individual constellation depends on the individual's state of consciousness, the collective constellation on the corresponding state of consciousness of human groups.

3. The charge of the archetype is manifested in a kind

of magnetic pull on the conscious mind, which, however, is not at first recognized. It takes the form of a vague emotional activity, which may swell into violent psychic agitation.

4. Attracted by the charge, the light of consciousness falls on the archetype; the archetype enters the actual psychic area, it *is perceived*.

5. When the archetype as such is "touched by consciousness," it can manifest itself either on the "lower," biological plane and take form, for instance, as an expression of instinct or as an instinctual dynamism, or on the "higher," spiritual plane as an image or idea. In the latter case the raw material of imagery and meaning are added to it, and the *symbol* is born. The *symbolic guise* in which it becomes visible varies and changes according to the outward and inward circumstances of the individual and the times. The encounter with the consciousness of a collectivity and its problems gives rise to collective symbols (e.g., mythologems); contact with an individual consciousness and its problems gives rise to individual symbols (as, for example, the image of a witch with the features of one's own mother).

6. The symbol acquires a certain degree of autonomy in its confrontation with the conscious mind.

7. The meaning with which the symbol is "pregnant" more or less compels the conscious mind to come to terms with it. This may occur in the most diverse ways—either spontaneously, through contemplation, representation, interpretation, etc., or else in the course of analysis.

8. The symbol may

a) be brought closer to the conscious mind by understanding and be felt and recognized as in some degree belonging to the ego, but without being wholly fathomed, so that it continues to be "alive" and effective;

b) be completely fathomed and explored. Then it seems wholly integrated with the ego and assimilated by the conscious mind, but it loses its "life" and efficacy, and becomes a mere allegory, a "sign," or a conceptually unambiguous content of consciousness;

c) not be understood at all: it may confront the ego consciousness as an expression of a complex hidden, so to speak, behind it, as a hostile foreign body, split off from it and causing a dissociation in the psyche. It then becomes an *autonomous splinter psyche*, which can make itself felt in the form of "spirits," hallucinations, etc., that is, in all kinds of neurotic and psychotic symptoms.

* *

Insofar as the "nucleus" of the complex is conceived as a dynamic "nodal point" in the structure of the collective unconscious, it may be equated, in regard to its nature and operation, with the archetype. But insofar as its "nucleus" is linked, in the course of the individual's life, with feeling-toned associations, and proliferates into a more or less autonomous psychic structure, it represents a psychic factor *sui generis*, which may appear in perceptible form, e.g., as a *symptom*, but which we shall do well to distinguish from both the symbol and the archetype. The second definition of the complex here given is the usual one, and depth psychology generally uses the term in this sense.

Since the complex usually denotes something nonperceptible, while the term symbol usually designates something "image-like," a clear distinction is advisable on this point, too. The dividing lines, to be sure, are not always clearly recognizable. One often speaks of complexes of a symbol-like and of symbols of a complex-like character, according to their particular shading.

In principle, according to Jung, complex and symbol are equivalent in many respects; i.e., insofar as both are rooted in an archetypal nucleus of meaning and in the collective unconscious. Thus there is some justification for using the terms archetype, complex, and symbol interchangeably in regard to their essential meaning—as Jung has done. If a finer differentiation is to be made and more exact boundary lines are to be drawn, we must distinguish between the complexes of the collective unconscious which, properly speaking, must be included among the archetypes or in certain cases the symbols, and those arising from the personal unconscious, in which a certain number of symbols from the collective unconscious lie hidden behind the individual manifestation and can be divested of their "individual covering." Most complexes of the personal unconscious must, however, be interpreted as signs or symptoms.

The difference between the various types of effects and meanings of complex and symbol in the healthy and the sick results not from their content but from the state of the ego consciousness confronting them and from the way in which this consciousness deals with them. The healthy man experiences and assimilates them with relative ease. He can overcome them as "disturbing factors" in the psychic economy, resolve the conflict, and make them fruitful as "catalysts" for his process of psychic development, as shown under 8 a) and b). In the sick man they become carriers of symptoms and images expressing his conflicts and lead to the difficulties and dangers mentioned under 8 c). Even though Jung, in accordance with the general usage, employs the term "complex" chiefly in its medical, that is, in the last-mentioned sense, a close scrutiny of his whole theory will show unmistakably that for him the complex cannot be regarded in itself as a disturber of the psychic health, but is so only within a definite constellation; and the same is true of the "symbol."

In addition to the role played by complex and symbol in the healthy and the sick, we must also consider their function in a third group of individuals, namely, creative men or artists. For the artist, complexes and symbols are not material to be exploited for his own psychic development; rather, they are the occasion and substance of his process of artistic creation and make him the guide, the authentic spokesman of the unexpressed but eternally and profoundly vital forces in the souls of mankind.

*   *

If we look back over the ground we have just surveyed, we behold a magnificent panorama of interrelated psychic meanings and the mysterious and autonomous "order" they create in a world of infinitely complex and varied activity. Symbols and complexes come and go; eternally unfolding, moving, and changing, they set their stamp on the life of the psyche, only to sink back again into the primordial womb of the unconscious, returning to their invisible archetypal forms of existence, until the time becomes ripe for them to emerge once more. In their un-differentiated state they bear within them salvation and doom, good and evil, health and sickness, and every con-ceivable pair of opposites. It is the task of the conscious mind, as the ordering and understanding principle in man, to help one or the other of these aspects to become opera-tive, and to add its sense- and form-giving energy to the indifferent sway of our primordial psychic nature, in order that neither instinct nor intellect, but a spirit that surveys them both, may keep the psyche in balance. This is a task which once again—this time by virtue of Jungian psychology—confirms the conscious mind in that status of pre-eminence and dignity which was accorded it by Creation itself, for it is "man's capacity for consciousness [which] alone makes him man."[89]

[89] "On the Nature of the Psyche," par. 412.

II. ARCHETYPE AND DREAM

The dream is a little hidden door in the innermost and most secret recesses of the soul, opening into that cosmic night which was psyche long before there was any ego consciousness, and which will remain psyche no matter how far our ego consciousness may extend. . . . All consciousness separates; but in dreams we put on the likeness of that more universal, truer, more eternal man dwelling in the darkness of primordial night. There he is still the whole, and the whole is *in him,* indistinguishable from nature and bare of all egohood.—Jung, "Die Bedeutung der Psychologie für die Gegenwart"[1]

---

[1] In *Wirklichkeit der Seele,* p. 49. ["The Meaning of Psychology for Modern Man," C. W. 10, here tr. R.F.C.H.]

Fig. 1. Night, Sleep, Death, and Dream

Night, clad in the "mantle of the stars," holds in her arms the twins,
death (the dark child) and sleep (the fair child). Dream flies down,
in his left hand an ivory wand as symbol of the false dreams, in his
right hand a horn as symbol of the true, good dreams. Woodcut from
Cartari, *Le Imagini de i dei de gli antichi* (Lyons, 1581).

INTRODUCTION

Ever since man has possessed self-knowledge, dreams, those messengers from the nocturnal half of life, have been carriers of the intrapsychic process, in which past, present, and future contents can take form with an inimitable richness of imagery and meaning. Hence the realm of dreams is the psychic area where we most frequently encounter archetypal themes. Here they appear in strangely impressive images and symbols, events and sequences. Often they put the conscious mind in a state of rapture that it cannot resist; for it is at the mercy of the numinous action of the archetypal images.

Most dreams containing archetypal themes also include other contents stemming from the personal unconscious. Dreams of a purely archetypal character are relatively rare. They always appear under special circumstances and, quite aside from the enduring subjective impression that they leave behind, reveal their significance in a plastic form which often attains poetic power and beauty. It is not for nothing that certain primitive peoples called them "big dreams"[2] in contradistinction to the "little dreams" concerned with less important everyday problems. They embody the contents of the collective unconscious, the "objective psyche" and its suprapersonal representations, which give expression to universally human or, in rare cases, to cosmic problems and ideas.

The archetype is operative even when the conscious

---

[2] Among primitive peoples only the "big dreams" are interpreted, for they concern not the individual alone, but the whole tribe.

mind does not understand it. It speaks in images that are common to all men and that rest in the creative, primordial ground of every psyche. For in the world of images the individual factor ceases to be anything more than a metaphor and becomes, as in myth, a copy of the universally valid, the eternally human.

"Archetypal products are no longer concerned with personal experiences but with general ideas, whose main significance lies in their intrinsic meaning and not in any personal experience and its associations."[3]

In the archetypal image love and hate, birth and death, courtship and separation, transformation and sacrifice, etc., appear in their transpersonal, universally human aspect, which transcends everything that is purely individual and reaches out beyond the preoccupations of the limited ego. "These [archetypal] dreams," says Jung, "occur mostly during the fateful phases of life, in early youth, puberty, at the onset of middle age (36 to 40), and within sight of death,"[4] i.e., in situations that apply to all men. They indicate that the psyche of the dreamer has got into a situation where it requires the help of the unfalsified voice of nature as it manifests itself in the archetypal images. At the turning point of middle life, for example, the reality of death may be brought home to a man by an archetypal dream, showing him unmistakably that he can no longer exclude it from his consciousness without injury to his psyche. For—in the interest of psychic self-regulation— every maladjustment, one-sidedness, eccentricity, obstruction, deviation, and disorientation of conscious life is compensated in dreams, often with seismographic accuracy and delicacy. Often the dream represents, as it were, an ingen-

[3] "The Nature of Dreams" (C. W. 8), par. 555.
[4] Ibid.

ious attempt to communicate to the psyche, in the language of images, an insight which happens to be needed just then, and which serves to establish a new balance. This is just as true of the dreams arising from the subjective and personal sphere, the "little dreams," as it is of the "big dreams" stemming from the objective, collective area of the psyche. Both contribute the compensatory insight that makes for better adjustment, the "little dreams" in respect to everyday life and the environment, the "big dreams" in regard to the typical, suprapersonal, universally human problems that transcend the ego. Thus, for example, the appearance of a mandala symbol in a dream may, through its implications of order and wholeness, exert a compensatory action on a chaotically disordered consciousness; it may work toward integration and help to restore the equilibrium.[5] For, as Jung says, the mandala communicates "the sensing of a center of personality, a kind of central point within the psyche, to which everything is related, by which everything is arranged, and which is itself a source of energy."[6]

The interpretation of archetypal dreams often involves considerable difficulties, because the personal associations that might help to explain them are usually few or wholly lacking. The dreamer is shaken by his inner images, he is astonished and often confused, but they suggest nothing, or only nonessentials, to him. Very frequently he understands neither their language nor their meaning. The whole dream strikes him as impenetrable; and even those who are no strangers to the language of the unconscious are often unable to relate their dreams meaningfully to

[5] Cf. "A Study in the Process of Individuation" and "Concerning Mandala Symbolism" (C. W. 9, i).
[6] "Concerning Mandala Symbolism," par. 634.

themselves. The affective component of the dream stirs the dreamer's emotions and bars the way to associations. For the dream expresses itself in strange, often mythological images. From the treasure house of the psyche it draws forth unusual shapes and figures, for the most part numinously charged. The best way to understand them is to go back to the world of collective images contained in legends and fairytales, in myths and poetry, or in the cultural and religious symbols of human history—the world in which dragon and serpent, treasure and cave, tree and blossom, gods and demons have their home and from which they speak to us in imperishable symbols.

For the interpretation of such dreams Jung has worked out a method of his own, namely the method of *amplification*. The various dream elements are "amplified" by related images and symbols which, by suggesting possible meanings, show the way to the actual meaning. The analogies employed are chosen regardless of epoch or cultural sphere; they may be either individual or collective in origin. The one essential criterion is that they should be utterances or creations of the human psyche which exhibit a common or similar meaning. Once understood in the light of these analogies, each element in the dream is examined in relation to those adjacent to it. In the end the whole dream is considered as a unit. If the intrinsically non-perceptible archetype, the underlying "primordial pattern," is concretized in a definite image which "presents" itself to consciousness in the dream, then the method of amplification, by adducing and comparing analogous archetypal images and symbols based on the same pattern, may point to the common factor that will confirm the presumed meaning.[7] Thus by painstaking detail work the probable

[7] Cf. Diagram XIV, p. 102, in my book, *The Psychology of*

sense of the dream may be deciphered. In the case of dreams containing only a few archetypal motifs or none at all, "objective amplification" will not suffice and "subjective amplification" will also be required. Here the dreamer must supply personal associations from his own biography, if the meaning of the dream is to be made clear to him.

Without exact knowledge of the dreamer's conscious attitude and without the context, provided by him, of his personal associations, no dream that does not disclose purely archetypal material can be satisfactorily interpreted. It must also be stressed that every interpretation is at first merely a hypothesis and that a number of additional criteria are needed before it can be regarded as valid and definitive. It will be relevant to know, for example, how the dreamer takes the interpretation: will he be moved by it, will he agree with it, will he receive it as a kind of revelation? And will it be confirmed by subsequent dreams? As a rule a single dream expresses only a partial aspect or only the immediately pressing problem of the dreamer's psyche. Only a considerable number of dreams can lend certainty and make it possible to correct errors in interpretation.

Thus a dream relating to something collective and timeless can be elucidated by "objective amplification," but it will provide only limited enlightenment and help in connection with the problems of the dreamer's personal, everyday life. The archetypes are without individual meaning; we must take the individual with all his personal troubles as the starting point, if we are to provide a sound

---

C. G. *Jung* (London, 1951), (p. 112, New Haven edn.), showing the individual archetypes represented in a dream and the connections between them.

interpretation applying to the particular dreamer, or reject a false one. Of course a dream comprising universal elements along with the personal ones can, in this respect, be interpreted even without "subjective amplification." We can pick out and interpret all motifs of a purely archetypal nature, but *only these*. This interpretation will disclose certain facts which by inference may permit us to form some opinion of the dreamer's momentary psychic situation, because they stand in a compensatory relation to it. But essentially such an interpretation is concerned with contents far removed from consciousness, in which the individual appears as a member of the species or of a greater or lesser collectivity.

Hence an archetypal dream must always be considered in its twofold aspect: what does it say in regard to the individual who has dreamed it, and what does it say in regard to the human collectivity? Every interpretation will deal first of all with the dreamer and his personal life. But in contrast to the so-called "little" dreams, the archetypal dream will point beyond this individual interpretation; according to the relative universality of its content, it will be relevant to many or to all men. Consequently some knowledge of the dreamer's present state of consciousness—supplied, for example, by psychotherapeutic work—will always be a prerequisite to sound interpretation, even if the dreamer can provide no personal associations.

"The unconscious is a cunning and skillful craftsman selecting just the symbol needed for the individual at the special time, but the value of the symbol is not a fixed and definite thing in itself. It lies in the relation of the symbol to the dreamer."[8]

[8] Frances G. Wickes, *The Inner World of Childhood* (1927), p. 308.

We are obliged to restrict ourselves to the archetypal content of a dream in dealing with most of the dreams handed down in history, or with those contained in myths, legends, or in the Bible, for no personal context is available. Still, such a context can be replaced in some cases (in connection, for example, with historical or literary dreams)[9] by biographical data that may have come down to us or by a careful examination of the *Zeitgeist* which influenced the dreamer. On the other hand, this limitation is inevitable with a particular category of dreams, namely, those of children, for as a rule the little dreamers have no associations to offer.

"The unconscious psyche of the child," says Jung, "is truly limitless in extent and of incalculable age. The dreams of three- and four-year-old children . . . are so strikingly mythological and so fraught with meaning that one would take them at once for the dreams of grown-ups, did one not know who the dreamer was. They are the last vestiges of a dwindling collective psyche which dreamingly reiterates the perennial contents of the human soul."[10]

And since the child psyche is still completely interwoven with its primal source; and since, as with primitives, magnificent, unexpected archetypal images often spring forth from their depths, the dreams of children provide particularly suitable material for the investigation of the nature and operation of the archetypes.

"Childhood is important," says Jung, "not only because various warpings of instinct have their origin there, but because this is the time when, terrifying or encour-

[9] See M. L. von Franz, "Der Traum des Descartes" (1952), and Aniela Jaffé, "Bilder und Symbole aus E. T. A. Hoffmanns Märchen 'Der goldene Topf' " (1950), p. 239.

[10] Jung, introduction to Wickes's *Analyse der Kinderseele,* in *The Development of Personality* (C. W. 17), pp. 44 f.

aging, those farseeing dreams and images appear before the soul of the child, shaping his whole destiny."[11]

* *

The child's dream considered below[12] is a remarkable illustration of what has been said because it provides a classic picture of the amazing image-making faculty of the psyche. Once again we can infer the profound meaning of the dream only by interpreting the archetypal images and symbols that occur in it. Little is known about the dreamer; nor has it been possible to obtain personal, subjective associations. Correction or amplification by means of the series to which this dream belonged was also impossible, partly because the other dreams were not available and partly because interpretation of a whole series would have carried us too far for our present purpose. Even so, this dream is sufficiently complete and well-rounded to be considered by itself. At all events its limited individual meaning can be guessed intuitively or worked out hypothetically in the form of inferences, even though we must dispense with the ultimate corroboration of our judgment—namely, the agreement of the dreamer. Insofar as every archetype embodied in symbols is "two-faced," i.e., represents not only factors already developed but also factors in process of becoming, it is oriented toward the future as well as the present. Thus we shall also have to consider its anticipatory aspect.

On this subject Jung writes: "Insofar as tomorrow is already contained in today, and all the threads of the future are already laid down, a deeper knowledge of the

[11] "On Psychic Energy" (C. W. 8), par. 98.
[12] The dream comes from the collection of Professor Jung, to whom it was given, along with the other dreams of the series, by the child's father after her death. I wish to express my thanks to Professor Jung for permitting me to work with it.

present might render possible a moderately farsighted prognosis of the future. . . . Just as memories that have long since fallen below the threshold are still accessible to the unconscious, so also are certain very fine subliminal combinations that point forward, and these are of the greatest significance for the future events insofar as the latter are conditioned by our psychology. . . . These might become the object of a refined psychological syntheticism that knew how to follow the natural currents of libido [but would not be accessible to a purely analytical method —J.J.]. This we cannot do, or only badly; but it happens easily enough in the unconscious, and it seems as if from time to time, under certain conditions, important fragments of this work come to light, at least in dreams, thus accounting for the prophetic significance of dreams long claimed by superstition. Dreams are very often anticipations of future alterations of consciousness."[13]

An interpretation on the object level is also impossible. For the dream contains no persons or figures who stand in a vital and immediate relationship to the dreamer and would therefore have to be considered in their material rather than symbolic reality. By their very nature archetypal dreams are primarily representations of an inner, purely psychic world, and not of a concrete, outward one.

The following attempt at interpretation is an illustration of Jung's method of getting at the meaning of a dream by amplification; it indicates a method of dealing with archetypal material, though in this form, of course, it could not be used for practical psychotherapeutic purposes. In the living process of an analysis such an investigation can be carried out only in its broad outlines; it can never be enriched with all this stratified and ramified

[13] *Symbols of Transformation* (C. W. 5), pp. 50 f., n. 18.

material: not only because the dreamer would very likely be unable to see the forest for the trees, but also because few analysts would be capable of producing impromptu at an analytical sitting such a wealth of amplification as is indicated and possible when there is time to select and deal carefully with the relevant parallels.

The difference in the methods of interpretation of Freud and Jung, and in their evaluation of dream motifs, is particularly evident in connection with archetypal dreams. Freud limited his investigations of dreams to the realm containing the biographical data of the dreamer, which Jung calls the "personal unconscious." Though Freud noted the existence of the material of the "collective unconscious" (as archaic vestiges), he did not take it into consideration. He did not adopt the concept of the archetype, and symbol did not mean to him what it means to Jung. For him the manifest dream content was not the decisive factor, as it is for Jung, but on the contrary the "latent" content, hidden behind the "dream façade." It is hidden by the dream elements, which serve as "cover figures" and can be laid bare and interpreted only by the method of causally determined "free association."[14] An archetypal dream such as that mentioned above provides a particularly appropriate and valuable basis for understanding the material of the unconscious on the symbolic level, a method of thought and interpretation particularly characteristic of the Jungian doctrine. In Jung's view,

[14] Freud makes an exception in certain cases, apparently in those where the meaning of a dream evades interpretation by a causal and reductive chain of associations. For he writes: ". . . our interpretative activity is in one instance independent of these associations—if, namely, the dreamer has employed *symbolic* elements in the content of the dream. In such cases we make use of what is, strictly speaking, a second and auxiliary method of dream-interpretation." *The Interpretation of Dreams* (Standard Edition), IV, 241 n.

the unconscious bases of dreams and fantasies only *seem* to be infantile memories. In reality they are *"primitive or archaic thought-forms, based on instinct,* which naturally emerge more clearly in childhood than they do later. But they are not in themselves infantile, much less pathological. . . . So also the myth, which is likewise based on unconscious fantasy processes, is, in meaning, substance, and form, far from being infantile or the expression of an autoerotic or autistic attitude, even though it produces a world picture which is scarcely consistent with our rational and objective view of things."[15]

In the dream Jung discerns a kind of *Gestalt,* a more or less rounded totality, similar in structure to a drama. The course of the dream can be broken down and its elements grouped according to the outline of a classical drama. The *exposition,* in which the *scene* of action and the *dramatis personae* are introduced, is followed by the *peripeteia:* the plot is woven, the knot is tied, the action approaches a *climax,* a turning point. Thereupon the *lysis* takes place. In it is manifest the result of the dream work, the conclusion which in a sense provides a solution to the problem in question. This drama-like structure can be discerned in the ensuing child's dream. Development, climax, and solution follow in swift succession, communicating an insight into the workshop of the soul, where the archetypes inexorably weave the destiny of man and creation.

* *

Dreams come and go as they please. Their meaning is often obscure, their purpose unknown. They rise up and bring with them images and truths, which amaze us by

[15] *Symbols of Transformation,* pp. 28-29.

their profundity and often surpass the power of human understanding. But the imagination can create nothing which does not already lie embedded in the depths of the psyche. And if man is able to imagine the divine and cosmic order, it is because he himself forms a part of it— *pars pro toto.*

THE DREAM OF THE BAD
ANIMAL

The dream that I shall here attempt to interpret was that
of an eight-year-old girl, who died of scarlet fever about
a year later. It was the last in a series of dreams recorded
by the child in a notebook which she gave her father as a
Christmas present. She herself entitled it "The Dream of
the Bad Animal." Here is the dream:

*"Once in a dream I saw an animal that had lots of
horns. It spiked up other little animals with them. It wrig-
gled like a snake and that was how it lived. Then a blue
fog came out of all the four corners, and it stopped eating. Then God came, but there were really four Gods in
the four corners. Then the animal died, and all the animals
it had eaten came out alive again."*[1]

At the very first glance one has a feeling that this dream
takes its place among the "big dreams" known to us from
the literature. Of course it is not to be classified, for
example, with the prophetic dreams of a medicine man,
from which one could infer future events affecting the
whole tribe. It is a "big dream" in the sense that it directly
discloses a kind of "world vision," a profound nucleus of
thought, and seems to reveal such a philosophical or cosmic truth as we find in old legends and fairy tales. Basically it seems more like a vision than a dream. It is like a

[1] Cited by Jung in his seminar on children's dreams (1939/40) and
mentioned in "A Study in the Process of Individuation" (C. W.
9, i), par. 623. In those citations the child's age is given as ten;
through private information, it is known that she was eight.

Fig. 2.

The Snake as a Symbol of the Passage of Time

The small snakes falling from the belly of the large snake
represent the various segments of time. Woodcut from
Chr. Cotterus Silesius, *Lux in Tenebris* (1657).

delicate oriental painting: indistinct contours, a few
blurred spots of color, here and there a brush stroke. But
if we immerse ourselves in the picture, the vacant background comes to life and takes on a fullness that threatens
to burst the frame. A varicolored diversity of forms and
figures emerges, and condenses into an image that moves
us and amazes us with its power.

The dreamer is not included in the action, which unrolls
before her like a color film. She records it in a cool, matter-
of-fact, almost disinterested tone, as though speaking of

some remote event which neither touches nor concerns us, but which we follow with the great, amazed, perhaps somewhat frightened eyes of a child. But it is not only the dreamer who stands in no perceptible relation to the dream action; man himself plays no part in it. This is perhaps the chief reason why the dream gives so strong an impression of remoteness from everything human and individual; it is a confrontation of animal and God. It is this total absence of man as an active or even as a passive participant that gives the dream its mood: the cool, awesome mood of the primeval, prehuman times when "the Spirit of God moved upon the face of the waters."[2] The subhuman and the superhuman, animal and God, face one another, naked and implacable. Primal matter and primal spirit clash, locked in the combat of death and birth that has been going on since time immemorial; it is the drama of life eternally dying and eternally reborn. The stage on which this struggle has been enacted since the dawn of history is the "inner space" of the human psyche, whose different aspects appear as the protagonists in the drama of the psyche.

* *

A closer study of the archetypal images or elements contained in the dream will, it is hoped, provide proof of our assertions. The dream—and Jung has found this to be true of most dreams—represents an actual drama in condensed and simplified form and readily lends itself to a breakdown according to the order underlying the classical drama.

The results of a breakdown according to the Jungian classification would be more or less as follows:

[2] Genesis 1 : 2.

Place:	Unbounded dreamland; the space encompassing the universe, and its four corners.
Time:	Once upon a time: timeless eternity.
Dramatis Personae:	The bad horned animal, the little animals, the blue fog, God in the form of the four Gods.
Exposition:	The bad animal with the many horns spikes up the little animals and eats them, and wriggles like a snake.
Peripeteia:	"Then a blue fog came out of all the four corners, and [the animal] stopped eating."
Climax:	"Then God came, but there were really four Gods in the four corners."
Lysis:	"Then the animal died, and all the animals it had eaten came out alive again."

In addition to this breakdown into the usual stages of development, still another, following from its peculiar structure, forces itself on our attention. I have in mind a twofold division into a kind of lower and upper, "earthly" and "heavenly" action. The fact that only animals and Gods appear in the dream makes the tension of opposites inherent in it particularly striking. In the first part the big bad animal and the little animals dominate the whole scene. In the second part God and the Gods appear and the bad animal is shorn of its power. We have then a conflict between animal and God, evil and good, darkness and light, matter and spirit, or whatever else these primordial opposites may have been called from the earliest

142

times. They existed from the beginning; they came into being on the second day of creation when God separated the "lower waters" from the "upper waters" and, shattering the unity of creation, established antithetical fields of energy. Ever since then all life has been enacted in those fields. And today they still contain the dynamic tension of all being, just as they did when the Creator, full of foreboding, paused to rest and for once was unable to say confidently, as on the other days, that "it was good." For in this separation lies the conflict, the rift, which runs through man and threatens to rend him apart, but which ultimately provides the impetus for the movement that transcends it and bridges it over.

Thus the "upper waters" became heaven and the "lower waters" became the earth. And then began the great struggle between the two, which endures to this day. For in these two principles, in the conflict and opposition between them—one might call them the archetypes of the first great tension of opposites, whether they bear the names matter and spirit, day and night, or male and female—lies the whole drama of creation and human destiny. From time immemorial the opposites have never ceased to exert their influence on man, and an endless chain of myths, legends, and mysteries still bears witness to their unbroken power.

If we now venture to assert that the "Bad Animal" of our dream is a symbol, a personification of the instinctual, dark "lower waters," our contention is supported by a number of astonishing analogies. By way of testing it, let us apply the method of "objective amplification" to the animal.

The hermaphroditic aspect of the animal

In the dream the animal is not named, nor is it described with any precision. We are told only that it has "lots of horns" with which it "spikes up other little animals" in order to eat them, and that it wriggles like a snake.

The first thing that strikes us is that the animal itself —and not only the dream as a whole—seems to combine antithetical characteristics. As a wriggling, snakelike creature it indubitably belongs to the damp, cold element; but its horns connect it with the fiery, hot element of penetrating passion. The animal's wriggling body may therefore be designated as a kind of snake and as a darkly chthonic, feminine-passive, devouring earth symbol, which is complemented by the active, masculine aspect of the horns. Thus the animal seems to be a primordial, cosmogonic monster, a symbol of the *prima materia*, which in keeping with its nature was almost always designated as bisexual. According to Jung, "the antithetical nature of the *ens primum* is an almost universal idea."[3] In Egyptian mythology Nun, the moist original substance, the "generative primal matter," both male and female by nature, was also invoked as "Amon, the primordial water which was in the beginning" and as "the father of fathers, the mother of mothers."[4] Many monsters were said to combine male and female attributes. Possibly Behemoth and Leviathan should be seen as a single monster; for Leviathan is called lord of the waters and female, while Behemoth is termed lord of the desert and male, perhaps an indication that in an older tradition the two were once a hermaphroditic being and were separated only in a

[3] *Psychology and Alchemy*, p. 318, n. 38.
[4] *Symbols of Transformation*, p. 240.

later myth.[5] Tiamat, the Babylonian primordial mother, is often depicted as bisexual, like the still undivided "hermaphrodite that was in the beginning"[6] in the symbolism of alchemy.

The existence of this duality and polarity (animal and God, Above and Below) not only in the dream as a whole, but also in the animal itself with its earthly-passive and fiery-active qualities, leads us to conclude that this is no ordinary animal but one of those mythical monsters which represent the symbolic embodiment of a totality, in this case the totality of one half of the world, the "lower world." In psychological terms this would mean the world of the instincts and drives, i.e., of the psyche that is associated with biological life.

The bilateral nature of fabulous animals is something characteristic of primordial times; consequently such animals always belong to the deepest realm of the unconscious and when in dreams they rise up out of its darkness they bring with them all the horror of primordial experiences. For they have their origins in the time when water was regarded as the beginning of the cosmos, as, for example, on the first day of the Creation in the Old Testament, or when water was thought to be the "*anima mundi*" of which the alchemists said: "*Aqua est vas nostrum.*"[7] In their symbolic language, the animals belonging to this primordial world were also symbols of the "matrix," the receptive feminine principle, of the alchemical "*vas,*" the "krater," the "vessel,"[8] hence representatives of the in-

[5] J. F. H. Gunkel, *Schöpfung und Chaos in Urzeit und Endzeit* (1895), p. 63.

[6] *Psychology and Alchemy*, pp. 281-82.

[7] Ibid., p. 227, n.

[8] *Von den Wurzeln des Bewusstseins*, pp. 162 f. ["Some Observations on the Visions of Zosimos," C. W. 13.]

exhaustible multiplicity of the Great Mother, in whom the male principle is not yet operative, of the Great Mother as symbol of the deepest realm of the unconscious, where the opposites, male and female, are not yet separate.[9]

Dragon and snake

As we draw in material for amplification, the fabulous primordial beast that undoubtedly deserves first mention is the dragon. In the very oldest traditions it was regarded as the personification of the destructive as well as the life-giving power of water. The dragon was long believed to be at the beginning of all human development—the story of man was the story of his attempts to free himself from the dragon's power. The even numbers, which in an ancient conception signified the feminine, the earth, the under-worldly, and evil, were often held to be personified by the dragon, or, as later in alchemy, by the *serpens Mercurii*, which represented the initial material of the *opus*. For Paracelsus the *prima materia* was an *"increatum,"* and this *increatum*, as in alchemy, was a bisexual serpent or a self-fecundating, self-generating dragon.[10] In psychological terms, "the dragon symbolizes the state of primordial unconsciousness, for this animal, as the alchemists say, likes to haunt 'caverns and tenebrous places.' "[11] The connection between the "beginning" of the world and the dragon is plastically represented in the Babylonian cosmogony. Tiamat, the dragon symbolizing the darkness of

[9] Cf. Erich Neumann, *Zur Psychologie des Weiblichen* (1953), and *The Great Mother* (1955).

[10] *Psychology and Alchemy*, p. 431.

[11] *Von den Wurzeln des Bewusstseins*, p. 186. ["Zosimos," here tr. R.F.C.H.]

the beginning, is often represented as a "raging serpent,"[12] who is conquered by Marduk, the sun hero. Thus the primordial matriarchal world is overcome by the bright masculine patriarchal world and the darkness of the unconscious is illumined by the rays of discriminating consciousness.

In ancient Egypt the dragon probably symbolized the great Nile floods with their fructifying and devastating consequences and for this reason was identified both with the god Osiris and with the goddess Hathor, or else in its beneficent aspect with Osiris and in its destructive aspect with his adversary Set. The Midgard Serpent of the Edda must also be regarded as a kind of dragon; it lies deep in the ocean surrounding the world, and indeed is this ocean itself.[13] The same is true of Rahab in the Book of Job, the "monster of the roaring seas," which only Yahweh can "assuage."[14] The oldest Sumerian mother goddess was a dragon.[15] Before the house of Medea lurks the vigilant dragon, and at night, we are told, the sun chariot is drawn not by horses as in the day, but by dragons.[16] The chariot of the mother goddess Demeter is also drawn by a dragon while she is in the underworld searching for her daughter Persephone.[17] Delphyne, the great enemy of Apollo, the "womblike giant serpent," which the god slew when he came to Delphi as a little boy, was likewise a dragon.[18] In early Greek mythology the dolphin was looked

[12] Gunkel, p. 28.
[13] Martin Ninck, *Wodan und germanischer Schicksalsglaube* (1935), p. 54.
[14] Gunkel, p. 36.
[15] Grafton Elliot Smith, *The Evolution of the Dragon* (1919), p. 231.
[16] E. Fuhrmann, *Das Tier in der Religion* (1922), pp. 39 f.
[17] Ibid., p. 39.
[18] Karl Kerényi, *The Gods of the Greeks* (1951), p. 136.

upon as a symbol of the child-bearing attribute of the sea.[19] The dolphin was said to be a sea beast provided with a uterus—this connotation being contained in the syllable "delph."[20]

In the Indian system of Kundalini Yoga, the Svadhisthana-Chakra of the watery region is inhabited by a dragon.[21] Among the most celebrated of dragon figures are the whale that swallowed Jonah and the Biblical Leviathan, who is described as a fire-spewing monster, a scaly sea serpent. According to the Old Testament: "He maketh the deep to boil like a pot; he maketh the sea like a pot of ointment. He maketh a path to shine after him; one would think the deep to be hoary."[22] Dragons were always mighty and feared, but often, as in China, they were held sacred and even worshiped for their power to bring water and rain. In some regions the dragon was originally identified with the crocodile, which was regarded as a bringer of rain, as a weather god.[23] Many peoples believed the dragon to be the creator of storms, the cause of floods and other upheavals. The storm rides on the dragon and brings about landslides and earthquakes.[24] Almost everywhere the dragon is related to the night, the darkness, the womb, the universal water.

Like the dragon, the snake, suggested by the "wriggling," belongs to the chthonic, cold, moist element of water, and to the material-feminine domain. In mythical

[19] Kerényi and L. M. Lanckoronski, *Der Mythos der Hellenen* (1941), p. 50.
[20] Ibid., p. 50.
[21] Arthur Avalon, *The Serpent Power* (1931), fig. 3.
[22] Job 41 : 31-32.
[23] E. Erkes, "Strohhund und Regendrache" (1930), p. 209.
[24] *Handwörterbuch des Deutschen Aberglaubens,* s.v. "Drache."

times it was regarded as the symbol of the ocean or the Jordan,[25] hence of moving water. It is generally regarded as a personification of the instinctual in its collective, impersonal, prehuman, and awesome aspect. According to the form and context in which it is found, it may be taken as a symbol "hostile to the light," as the embodiment of the "lower soul" in man, or as a symbol of the dark sexual drive. In this connection Freud calls it a phallic symbol, while Jung gives it a chthonic, feminine significance and relates it to the creative principle.

In the various mythologies snakes usually appear as companions or attributes of the great earth mothers. We encounter the serpent in connection with Hecate, the Greek moon goddess, and with the mother goddess Demeter. It is also closely related to water, and in many traditions it is connected with health-giving springs. It is an attribute of Asclepius, the chthonic healer god; indeed it is the god himself.[26] In the legend of paradise it is often represented with a woman's head. Among the Gnostics, particularly the Naassenes and Ophites, the serpent played a central role. According to a Gnostic source, "it is the moist substance . . . and nothing in the world, immortal or mortal, living or lifeless, can subsist without it."[27] Like the dragon, the serpent signifies the "initial material" in need of transformation, the *massa informis*, and as a primitive cold-blooded animal it stands for the instinctual unconscious in general, which by a slow process of development is to be spiritualized and ennobled. In alchemy it represents the transformative substance,

[25] Hans Leisegang, *Die Gnosis* (Kröner edn., 1924), p. 141.
[26] C. A. Meier, *Antike Inkubation und moderne Psychotherapie* (1949), pp. 72 ff.
[27] Leisegang, p. 141.

the alchemical Mercurius which symbolizes both the transformation process and its content.[28]

Serpent[29] and dragon symbolism presents well-nigh innumerable aspects, and it was possible to cite only a few that have some relevance to our dream. They are among the most frequent symbols appearing in the material of the unconscious, and they present a wide variety of meanings according to the context in which they appear.

The horn

We have briefly considered a few of the amplifications relating to a wriggling, snakelike creature. Now we apply the same method to the symbolism of the horn. The animal in the dream is said to have "lots of horns."

Horns are phallic symbols. They stand for the exact opposite of the moist, chthonic snake. In mythological times and among primitive peoples the horn was taken as an embodiment of the sun's rays, hence of an active, masculine, fiery principle. This active, solar principle is both creative and destructive. Sinking into the earth, the sunbeam can make the seed germinate, that is, it can fructify —a conception that has endured to our own day—but with its fire it can also sear and destroy life. Yet in whatever form we encounter the solar principle, it always plays the role of an "agent"; it always signifies strength and power. Consequently numerous deities bear horns; Michelangelo, for example, endowed Moses with horns as a symbol of his spiritual power. Alexander the Great was known as the two-horned and as a sign of his extraordinary power

[28] Cf. also *Psychology and Alchemy*, pp. 241 ff.
[29] See Erich Küster, *Die Schlange in der griechischen Kunst und Religion* (1913), which provides rich documentation on the subject.

was represented with ram's horns on his head; Julian the Apostate appeared on Roman coins as Serapis with a jagged crown, whose teeth symbolized penetrating rays.[30] Hathor, the Egyptian queen of chaos, also bears horns, and the ten horns of the beast in the vision of Daniel[31] signify the power of the kings of Rome and Greece.

The positive and negative aspects of the horn are attested in numerous traditions. The raging bull which gored the bodies of the first Christian martyrs in the Roman arena will remain forever a symbol of blind rage, destructive intensity, death-dealing power. The Hermetic philosophers, on the other hand, believed that the legendary unicorn had the power to consecrate water with its horn, to cleanse it from sin, and that this bore witness to its high creative quality. In Christian legend the unicorn is identified with the Holy Spirit which penetrated and fructified Mary's womb.[32] It played a similar role in the beliefs of the Gnostics and of some of the alchemists.[33] In Africa the unicorn designates the rank of princes and emperors and among certain tribes it was worshiped as a symbol of the sun.[34] Finally, there is the dragon of the Apocalypse with its seven heads and ten horns: "And the ten horns which thou sawest are ten kings, which have received no kingdom as yet; but receive power as kings one hour with the beast."[35]

The Devil as prince of darkness almost always bears horns, a conception that has been preserved down to our

[30] Cf. *Symbols of Transformation*, plate XXa.
[31] Daniel 7 : 7.
[32] *Psychology and Alchemy*, pp. 419 ff.
[33] "The Paradigm of the Unicorn," in *Psychology and Alchemy*, pp. 415 ff., in which may be found numerous illustrations of the motif.
[34] Fuhrmann, *Das Tier in der Religion*, p. 28.
[35] Revelation 17 : 12.

own day, although today he has acquired a somewhat gentler and more civilized exterior than in the Middle Ages, when he was generally conceived as a hideous monster with gaping jaws, ever ready to devour sinners.

The horned serpent

The dream does not tell us whether the animal had only one body or several, whether it had one or several heads, or where the horns were located. Here again a number of versions must be examined for their relevance.

Some of the many-headed dragons achieved immortal fame. We have all read about Ladon, the dragon which guarded the golden apples of the Hesperides,[36] and the Lernaean Hydra slain by Heracles—the water serpent with the many heads and the poison breath which pierced its victims like a horn.[37] There is one hypothesis that identifies the dragon with the many-headed octopus depicted on many Cretan vases,[38] and another that attributes several heads to Leviathan.[39] We are not told whether these many-headed snakes and dragons had horns; but there are others expressly accredited with horns of various shapes. The best known of these is the great seven-headed, ten-horned red dragon of the Apocalypse: "And the great dragon was cast out, that old serpent called the Devil."[40] Among the Pueblo Indians the horned serpent was a water spirit with a special religious significance.[41] "Wani," the Chinese and Japanese dragon, also bears horns;[42] and

[36] Kerényi, *The Gods of the Greeks*, pp. 51 ff.
[37] Ludwig Preller, *Griechische Mythologie* (1921), II, 444.
[38] Elliot Smith, *The Evolution of the Dragon*, p. 215 and fig. 24c and others.
[39] Gunkel, *Schöpfung und Chaos*, pp. 83 ff.
[40] Revelation 12 : 9.   [41] Elliot Smith, p. 91.
[42] Ibid., p. 103.

the semidivine Naga serpents included one variety, the
sea dragons, with human torso, horned head, and snakelike coils in place of legs.[43] Maya tradition speaks of an
alligator dragon with small horns, and indeed there is
a whole group of dragons bearing the horns of antelopes,
gazelles, or deer. In American Indian legend, there was a
dragon with antlers and wings, and in China the dragon was
often designated as a "celestial stag."[44]

Almost everywhere devil, dragon, and serpent are
equated. Gerard Dorn, a sixteenth-century alchemist, recognized the Devil himself in the *"serpens quadricornutus,"*
the four-horned serpent.[45] In Manichaean doctrine the
Devil ruled over the primeval waters: "He devoured and
consumed everything, spread devastation to right and left,
and descended into the depths, in all these movements
bringing down destruction and doom from above."[46] Are
we not reminded of the behavior of the "Bad Animal"
in the dream?

Impaling ("spiking up") and devouring

These two modes of action are characteristic of man
as well as animals. They are forms of action or reaction
which occur under definite circumstances and which embody archetypal modes of behavior.

Impaling is similar to boring, piercing, penetrating,
etc., and is closely related to the instrument employed,
pike, arrow, sword, spit, or dagger, in any case something
pointed, sharp, penetrating. In our case it is the horn that
possesses these attributes and does the "spiking." Trans-

---

[43] Ibid., p. 108.   [44] Ibid., pp. 91, 133.
[45] Jung, "Synchronicity" (C. W. 8), par. 962.
[46] Gunkel, p. 54.

posed into psychological terms, these may symbolize the passionate, active, forward-pressing, penetrating qualities of the psyche. In the Apocalypse the power of Christ's word is a sharp sword issuing from the mouth.[47] The lightning, too, because of its penetrating power, is often employed as a symbol of sudden and overwhelming love, whose blessed or annihilated victim is man. Zeus in the form of a lightning flash penetrated Semele with his love,[48] and from this union sprang Dionysus. And the phallic significance, which undoubtedly attaches to spiking or impaling, suggests a number of other aspects relating to the act of fecundation, to the penetrating intensity of libido or psychic energy, to blind instinct, unbridled desire, and similar phenomena.[49] The penetrating principle can take the most diverse forms; its action can be both destructive and fruitful; it is an "inciter" which promotes development or it may bring death and so provide the impetus to rebirth.

The alchemists spoke of a "penetrating Mercurius,"[50] a "spirit that is hidden in matter," and strove to extract it from the ore in order to gain possession of the "essential," the "spiritual matter," with which they believed that the imperfect state could be transformed into a perfect one. Thus the impaling of the "small animals" may have been a painful "fecundation," prerequisite to their subsequent resurrection; it may have the same significance here as dismemberment, *mortificatio*, etc., in alchemy. The horns would then be equivalent to the "dividing sword" or the "wounding spear," the *telum passionis*, the weapon of Mercurius in the alchemical *opus*,[51] to the

[47] Revelation 19 : 15.
[48] Kerényi, *The Gods of the Greeks*, pp. 256 f.
[49] *Symbols of Transformation*, pp. 64 f.
[50] *Psychology and Alchemy*, p. 285.
[51] Ibid., p. 284, fig. 150.

penetrating sunbeam, or to Mephisto's "key," with which Faust hoped to gain admittance to the realm of the Mothers. The horn would play the part of the *sperma mundi*, which kills by its intensity, but at the same time animates and fertilizes.

*   *

Being devoured or swallowed is also a widespread archetypal motif that may be found in innumerable legends, fairy tales, and myths. Its best-known prototype is the story of Jonah, swallowed up by the whale. The whale, as we have seen, is related to the dragon, which in turn often appears as symbol of water, of the ocean that swallows the sun and gives birth to it again. The witch who eats up children, the omnivorous ogre, the wolf that devours the kid, are typical fairy-tale figures of like meaning. Such alchemical conceptions as the lion that eats up the sun,[52] or Gabricus, who enters into the body of his sister and is there dissolved into atoms,[53] belong to this symbolism. In symbolical language, being devoured represents a kind of descent into the underworld, a sinking back into the womb, resulting in the extinction of consciousness, the death of the ego. Consciousness is engulfed by the darkness of the unconscious, which is also a parallel to the Terrible Mother, who represents the hungry maw of hell.[54] In functional and psychological terms, this means a sinking back of the libido into the unconscious. In order that the individual may be freed from its deadly embrace, a "rescue" is needed, such as is described in numerous stories of heroes. Jung writes: "Time is thus defined by the rising and setting

[52] Ibid., fig. 169.
[53] Ibid., p. 323.
[54] *Symbols of Transformation*, Pls. XVI, XXIIb, XXXIV, XXXVIII, LXII, figs. 30, 33.

sun, by the death and renewal of libido, the dawning and extinction of consciousness."[55] The journey to Hades, the Nekyia, engulfment by the beast of chaos: all represent death and the torments of hell, but at the same time they are forerunners of salvation and rebirth.

The dual psychological aspect of the animal

In order to understand the "Bad Animal" we must not only consider its parallels in myth, folklore, etc., but also and above all investigate its symbolical significance in the realm of the psyche. The Devil, in *Faust*, is said to be "a part of that power which would ever do evil, yet engenders good." This profound truth is particularly applicable to the realm of archetypes and symbols, for bipolarity is an essential part of their nature. In the still undivided whole, as well as in the pairs that have already been joined, all possibilities are present; and this is why archetypal images or symbols are so often bisexual.[56]

But this dual aspect applies not only to masculine and feminine, but also to positive and negative qualities. Serpents and dragons, those mighty symbols of darkness and evil, are also the guardians of gold and hidden treasures and miraculous springs. They represent the initial state which always contains hidden values, "golden seeds." The dragon who guarded the golden apples of the Hesperides, and Fafnir, the giant dragon who guarded the treasure of the Nibelungs, belong to this context. The Golden Fleece was guarded by a dragon, and Apollodorus tells us that one of the Lernaean Hydra's heads was of gold[57] and therefore immortal. As a sign of its divinity

[55] Ibid., p. 280.   [56] Cf. Part I, p. 95 f.
[57] Preller, *Griechische Mythologie*, II, 447.

the serpent Khnufis wore a crown of sunbeams, and Christ himself is likened in the New Testament to the "serpent of brass," which Moses set up in the desert as a safeguard against the "fiery serpents" that infested the region.[58] There is also a fable about a magical dragon stone to be found in the head of the dragon, and the blood of certain dragons was believed to make those who bathed in it invulnerable.[59]

Thus the snake not only signifies instinct, but also has another, magical, mystical-religious meaning. It is the expression of a particular state, a "libido analogue," or reflection of the dynamism of the psyche, representing the ceaseless flow of the psychic process. It is the quicksilver of the alchemists, the "serpens Mercurii" in man, whose psychic life drives forward, never resting, engulfing image after image in the chaos of its dark underworld, only to give them forth again, reborn and transformed. The annual casting of the snake's skin is an apt symbol for this. For the snake is on the one hand the "massa confusa," the "nigredo" (blackness), the "prima materia" itself that stands at the beginning of the alchemical process, while on the other hand, as in our dream, it is also the vessel in which the process of transformation takes place. It is a crucible, a cooking vessel like Zosimos' bowl-shaped altar,[60] or the great water basin in Poliphilo's dream,[61] in which men were immersed in order to be boiled or devoured. It is the belly of the whale where the heat is so

---

[58] Numbers 21 : 6-8; John 3 : 14.

[59] *Handwörterbuch des Deutschen Aberglaubens*, s.v. "Drache." (See also the legend of Siegfried, especially Wagner's treatment in *The Ring of the Nibelungs*.)

[60] "Transformation Symbolism in the Mass" (C. W. 11), pp. 225 ff.

[61] Linda Fierz-David, *The Dream of Poliphilo* (tr. 1950), pp. 81 ff.

great that the hero loses his hair,[62] a kind of giant uterus such as is represented by Noah's ark, in which, amid struggle and pain, the old is transformed into the new: the dragon's treasure, the transformed and purified psyche.

Thus we would seem to be justified in drawing a parallel between the "Bad Animal" in our dream and such a "giant uterus," the uterus of the Great Mother World, as it were, which devours and rebears, destroys life and bestows it.

* *

In the light of what has been said, it seems unmistakable that the wriggling "Bad Animal," spiking up other, little animals on its horns and devouring them, is an archetypal creature possessing numerous fellows in the "untrodden, never to be trodden,"[63] realm of the unconscious.

Some of the variations in which this archetype can take form have been shown by the amplifications cited above. But even the most painstaking attempt at a description and explanation can be no more than a translation into images of a different kind and can never do justice to the essence of the archetype.

The little animals

If we interpret the "Bad Animal" of our dream as a "giant uterus" or as the great "maw of the unconscious," the "little animals" may be regarded as the *prima materia*, the "raw material" of the psyche, which must first succumb to death before it can awaken, recast, to new and

[62] Leo Frobenius, *Das Zeitalter des Sonnengottes* (1904), I, 62.
[63] Goethe, *Faust*, Part II, Act I, "A Dark Gallery."

perhaps more differentiated, more nearly perfect, and more enduring life.

The impaled little animals are not described in the dream; we do not know what sort of animals they are. Perhaps they are no more than simple body substances, still unnamed and unclassified. If we view them as psychological functions, we might designate them as animated parts, functional components of the psyche. But they might equally well signify a kind of waste product, disintegrated, atomized elements of the psyche, autonomous psychic contents which, by passing through death in the womb of the unconscious, in the belly of the devouring monster, resurrect to new life and so achieve a new unity.[64] When the alchemists say that Gabricus enters the body of Beya and is there dissolved into atoms, this signifies a *mortificatio* of consciousness or the disappearance of the sun, the engulfment of its rays by the dark belly of night, which must precede its morning resurrection.[65] Moses called the stars the serpents of the desert, and the many snakes by which the Hebrews were bitten in their wanderings were personifications of evil powers, to combat which God commanded Moses to raise a great brass serpent on a pole and so break the disintegrating power of the many by the condensing power of unity.[66] But the "little ani-

[64] In view of the outcome of the dream and the dreamer's age, it seems wiser to judge them as not yet integrated and differentiated functional psychic qualities and possibilities, rather than as products of dissociation which, at an advanced stage of the process of disintegration, would lead to a dissolution of the personality into its psychic components, its complexes, for example, as can happen in schizophrenia.

[65] *Psychology and Alchemy*, p. 323.

[66] Numbers 21 : 6-8.
Gabricus is the spiritual principle of light and the Logos, which, like the Gnostic Nous, sinks down in the embrace of Physis. His

mals" may also be taken as units of time swallowed by the dark maw of the night, like the "pieces of the moon," which, when their time has come, emerge from the black sky and awaken to new being. Since archetypal motifs have several aspects, it follows that they also have several possible meanings.

To sum up, we might say that the part of the dream discussed so far embodies a psychic state in which the dark, instinctual aspect of the collective unconscious, symbolized by the archetypal image of the horned monster, "presents" itself to the little girl's dream consciousness and, in the devouring of the little animals, i.e., the destruction of many individual psychic components, shows its negative, life-destroying side. But at the same time— because in the realm of the psyche as elsewhere there can be no resurrection without death, no becoming without dying—the stage is set for the enantiodromia, the counterflow of energy that will activate the positive, spiritual aspect of the collective unconscious and bring about a turn in the intrapsychic struggle.

The blue fog or vapor

"Then a blue fog came out of all the four corners, and the animal stopped eating." The dark, instinctual flow of the "lower waters" is opposed by their mighty counterpart, the "upper waters," said to have "the spirit of the Highest . . . enclosed within them."[67] This is the nadir; a

---

death symbolizes the descent of the spirit into matter. Should the "little animals" be regarded as symbols of "spiritual atoms," of vehicles of light, or rather as evil instincts like the serpents in the desert? We do not know; we can only attempt to draw analogies that may make for a better understanding of the dream.

[67] *Psychology and Alchemy*, p. 268.

turn sets in. And so too in our dream: just when the affliction is greatest, God's help is nearest, arching high over the dark underworld like the blue dome of heaven. What happens here, very much as in "Liber Platonis Quartorum," the anonymous Harranite treatise, so acutely commented upon by Jung, is a transformation of the initial material ". . . up to the highest stage, where nature is transformed into the 'simple thing' which, in accordance with its own kind, is akin to the spirits, angels, and eternal ideas."[68] In other words, we have a rising of the "volatile, subtle body," known also as vapor, which for the alchemists of the sixteenth century symbolized the "intermediate realm between mind and matter," namely the realm of the psyche.[69] The ancients described the psyche as a "damp, cool breath," resembling in essence the living breath of God, which he breathed into the body of man, that had been formed of clay.[70] The Stoics taught that "the moving waters from the springs and lakes send up a sweet mild exhalation"[71] to feed the moon—which in their belief was closely connected with the psychic realm. And in the twenty-third book of the Iliad we read about the soul of the dying Patroclus: "For the soul was gone like smoke into the earth, twittering."[72]

Vapor is the "pneumatic body" of the alchemists, the "volatile substance." As water vapor in the air, it vividly represents the transformation from something corporeal

[68] Ibid., pp. 250-51, n. 51.

[69] Ibid., p. 266.

[70] Cf. Genesis 1 : 7. The beautiful Genesis mosaics in St. Mark's in Venice show how Adam, through the soul breathed into him by God, was transformed from a black clod of clay into a luminous human body.

[71] "Isis and Osiris," in Plutarch, *Moralia* (tr. F. C. Babbitt), p. 101.

[72] Tr. W. H. D. Rouse, p. 267.

into something seemingly incorporeal, like a gas or spirit.[73] From it arise the clouds, harbingers of rain and fertility. Thus fog or vapor is a kind of intermediary between Below and Above, the earthly and the celestial. At the famous oracle of Delphi the priestess Pythia sat on a brass tripod placed above a cleft in the earth from which vapors arose. It was in these vapors that the god Apollo revealed himself to her, from them that she derived her inspiration.[74] In the mythologies the helpful god often appears in a veil of mist. "Let mist be before me, mist behind me, and the good Lord himself above me," says a proverb from Bohemia.[75] In describing the Mercurial fountain,[76] Jung writes that the "two vapors" issuing from the jaws of two snakes initiate a process of sublimation or distillation whose purpose it is to purify the *prima materia* from the "*mali odores*" (foul smells) and from the "original blackness adhering to it," whereby a process of continuous transformation is instigated.[77] The fog rising from the four corners in our dream image serves the same purpose. It connects earth and heaven, the "lower process" with the approaching "upper process"; with its help the world of the *prima materia*, the world of the "Bad Animal" will purify itself and "evaporate." Thus the fog, mists, or vapors represent, so to speak, the four pillars supporting the higher powers that bring reversal and transformation.

* *

[73] Cf. "Concerning Mandala Symbolism" (C. W. 9, i), figs. 53 and 54, where the "souls of the calcinated *prima materia*" escape as vapors in the form of little men (*homunculi*).

[74] Kerényi, "Das Geheimnis der Pythia," in *Apollon*, p. 284.

[75] *Handwörterbuch des deutschen Aberglaubens*, VI, 99.

[76] "Psychology of the Transference" (C. W. 16), pp. 203 ff.

[77] Cf. also *Psychology and Alchemy*, fig. 134, p. 253, in which Mercurius Senex (or Saturn), i.e., lead, the *prima materia*, is boiled in a bath until the spirit escapes from the rising vapors and flies away in the form of a white dove (*pneuma*).

Innumerable meanings attach to "blue" in linguistic usage, and an elaborate symbolism has grown up around it. Here we can give only a few examples.

It seems appropriate to mention the connection between fog and the color blue in the expression *"einen blauen Dunst vormachen"*—"to give off a blue fog," i.e., to cast a mist before a person's eyes and "befog" him. Here the blue fog refers to unproved, meaningless, vaporous thoughts without reality and intended to mislead. But perhaps this aspect may be taken in another, more prospective sense; for it would seem to be part of the dream's purpose to diminish the terrifying aspect or even the reality of the monster, to throw a "blue fog" around it and so make it more bearable: the psyche would then be striving to depotentiate the chthonic-destructive side of the unconscious, symbolized by the wriggling beast, through the upward movement of a pneumatic-volatile substance directly opposed to it. The "blueness" of this substance should not, therefore, be regarded as a negative quality; it would suggest a process of spiritualization, a "sublimation," a kind of compensatory self-regulation of the psychic parallelogram of forces. And indeed we say: *"Er hat keinen blauen Dunst von einer Sache"*— "He hasn't got a blue fog of a thing"—meaning, he hasn't the foggiest notion of it. In this case, the "blue fog" must be taken as something positive. For, if the person in question had a "blue fog," he would be better informed. His lack of it implies the absence of a minimum of founded knowledge, i.e., a lack of intelligent activity on the part of his psyche.

Blue has always been regarded as the color of the spirit, the heavens, the upper world. In certain regions the soul rising upwards after death is called "a little blue smoke."[78]

[78] *Handwörterbuch des deutschen Aberglaubens,* I, 1367.

Blue is the color of most heavenly gods. In the Tyrol, for example, Christ was represented in a blue mantle in Palm Sunday processions,[79] and Mary, as Virgin Queen of Heaven, is often shown in a blue cloak. Because of her various blue attributes (veil, cross, ribbon, etc.) in early German paintings, she is often popularly referred to as the "Blue Lady."[80] Blue, because of its spiritual implication, was often regarded as a safeguard against evil spirits; it was employed in magical operations designed to ward off water demons, and this aspect also enters into our dream. The "blue flower of Romanticism"[81] is another indication of the symbolic value of blue; it stands for man's yearning for the sublime to the exclusion of all bestial urges. "Blue Monday"[82] is the fast day on which the faithful are bidden to abstain from all carnal pleasures, i.e., to spiritualize themselves.[83]

The color blue is highly esteemed in India, where it often appears as an attribute of the divine and eternal. Thus a "blue body" is the prerogative of Krishna alone,[84] and in the vision of the "four great gods" in the Tibetan Book of the Dead, the highest place is accorded to the Dharma-Dhātu shining in a blue light, the body of Buddha: "It is the aggregate of matter resolved into its primordial state which is the blue light. The Wisdom of the Dharma-Dhātu, blue in color, shining, transparent, glorious, dazzling, from the heart of Vairochana as the Father-

[79] Ibid., p. 1372.   [80] Ibid., p. 1263.

[81] The expression was coined by Novalis in his novel *Heinrich von Ofterdingen* (1802).

[82] H. F. Singer, *Der blaue Montag* (1917).

[83] In Swiss dialect the term *"machsch Blaue"* is employed for an unwarranted cessation of work.

[84] ETH Lectures, 1938/39, p. 91. [I.e., notes of a seminar given by Jung in German at Federal Polytechnical Institute, Zurich, privately mimeographed.]

Mother."[85] And in the water *chakra* (Svadhisthana), according to Kundalini Yoga, there dwells the divine Hari-Vishnu, whose body is of glittering blue and "magnificent to behold," for he has "the blue radiation."[86]

*   *

Like fog and mist, blue is related to the clouds and rain, hence to fertility, growth, and renewal. Blue gives a feeling of coolness like the night sky, of purity and clarity like the shimmering daytime firmament, of mistiness like the air, of transparency like the water. Blue is at once height—the heavens above—and depth—the water below. Like the mist it points both to the upper, divine realm and to the chthonic, lower realm. In India, the rain god Indra was besought in certain ceremonies to shake his blue, cloudy cloak in order to bring the rain. In China, the "azure, blue dragon" was looked upon as the most generous bringer of rain and as the highest in rank of all dragons.[87]

Thus the "blue fog" may be regarded as a sort of transition, as a "connecting link" between two realms of the unconscious psyche. It belongs both to the lower, "watery" realm and to the upper, "blue" realm, and meaningfully unites the two.

The four

In the timeless, spaceless dream image the "blue mists" rise up as though from the four corners of the universe: they form a vast frame composing the spaceless into a

[85] W. Y. Evans-Wentz, *The Tibetan Book of the Dead* (1957), p. 106.
[86] Arthur Avalon, *The Serpent Power*, pp. 359 ff.
[87] Elliot Smith, *The Evolution of the Dragon*, p. 109.

unity like the four angels of the Apocalypse who hold the winds at the four corners of the earth,[88] or like the four winds of heaven which "strove upon the great sea" in Daniel's vision.[89] The destructive action of a chthonic power in the unconscious is checked and eliminated by the appearance of pneumatic, spiritual counterforces on the four sides of the psychic area.

It is noteworthy that with the appearance of the "blue mists" the "Bad Animal" stops eating. Touched by the mysterious power of the quaternity which they represent, struck by the ordering law of their quadratic arrangement, it stops as though paralyzed. The negative flow of energy is halted and gives way to an activity of an entirely different kind. For it is highly significant that these "mists" are situated in all four corners and therefore can surround and contain the beast.

This marking off of the four corners, setting limits to the "disordered initial state," to the *massa confusa* of the unconscious psyche, symbolized by the devouring monster, gives rise to a first "order." As in ancient cults, a space is marked off within which the mystery of transformation can proceed. For in many religious conceptions the quaternity arranged in a square had a magical, protective quality, a numinous character, and a sacral significance.[90]

Four is an age-old symbol, probably going back as early as the Old Stone Age. It occurs in the image of the "four

[88] Revelation 7 : 1.

[89] Daniel 7 : 2.

[90] *Psychology and Alchemy*, p. 79, fig. 31: the city with its walls ordered in the form of a square as "*temenos*," and p. 103, fig. 50: the square citadel offering protection against spirits of disease, etc. Cf. also the description of the "heavenly Jerusalem" in the Book of Revelation and the symbolism of the "high cities," e.g., the "*Roma quadrata*" in antiquity.

rivers" of Paradise, the cradle of mankind. The four cardinal points of the horizon, the four phases of the moon, the four seasons, the four primary colors, etc., are fundamental elements in our experience of the world. Probably the structure and cell division of all organic matter are also based on this primordial law of fourness; it forms a natural pattern of order within all created matter. The quaternity of the elements as the basic substances of the world in the old natural philosophy, the four humors and temperaments in ancient medicine, have played an important role in the intellectual development of mankind. Examples might be multiplied indefinitely.[91]

According to the Gnostic view, the quaternity was the soul itself; it was the anthropos, the first mortal Adam, who consisted of the four elements.[92] But it was also the matrix for the birth of the second, the purified and immortal Adam.[93] The philosophers of the Middle Ages believed that the *prima materia* would have to be divided into four parts and that man's original nature, his blind instinctuality, would have to be sacrificed, in order that it might be reborn on a higher level. For Pythagoras the square was the symbol of the soul.[94] The Gnostic Marcus,

[91] A detailed exposition of the symbolism of the quaternity is impossible within the limits of this work. Of the compendious literature on the symbolism of numbers we might mention: A. W. Buckland, "Four as a Sacred Number" (1896); V. F. Hopper, *Medieval Number Symbolism* (1938); R. F. Allendy, *Le Symbolisme des nombres* (1948); F. C. Endres, *Die Zahl in Mystik und Glauben der Kulturvölker* (1935); L. Paneth, *Zahlensymbolik im Unbewussten* (1952). Jung devotes special attention to the problem of the quaternity or *tetraktys* in his "Psychology and Religion," *Psychology and Alchemy, Aion, Mysterium Coniunctionis*, etc.

[92] *Psychology and Alchemy*, p. 355.

[93] "Psychology and Religion" (C. W. 11), par. 94.

[94] Zeller, *Die Philosophie der Griechen*, III, ii, p. 120 (as cited in "Psychology and Religion" [C. W. 11], p. 72).

who followed Pythagoras in his number mysticism, related the four to Christ, since $1 + 2 + 3 + 4$ add up to ten, i.e., the numerical value of the first Hebrew letter of the name Jesus.[95] And the Barbelo-Gnostics derived their name and their philosophico-religious principle of the cosmos from the Hebrew words Barbe-Eloha, "God is in the four."[96] The quaternity occupied a position of fundamental importance in the alchemists' strivings for the *opus* and the "Philosophers' Stone."

Jung has found the quaternity to be the archetypal foundation of the human psyche. And with the theory of the four functions,[97] i.e., with the discovery of the significant role of the quaternity in the human psyche, whose archetypal basis he found it to be, Jung clarified a vast number of relationships and symbols. We know, for example, from Jung's researches and observations, that mandalas, those remarkable images for meditation found in oriental religions and also occurring frequently in the psychic development of the modern occidental, are based on the quaternity principle and may be regarded as symbols of the "primordial order" of the psyche. Both the production of mandalas and meditative immersion in them can awaken or express this "original order" that is potentially present in every psyche.

The important place assumed by the quaternity in our dream suggests its decisive significance for the dreamer's psyche. According to Jung, the appearance of four in a dream always symbolizes something very important that concerns the dreamer personally; it is, as it were, the crea-

[95] Leisegang, *Die Gnosis*, p. 338.
[96] Ibid., p. 186.
[97] The four aspects of psychological apprehension and orientation are described in Jung's *Psychological Types*.

tive background of a religious experience that has been vouchsafed to man in endless variations throughout his history.[98] For the depths of the collective unconscious still contain everything they ever contained and in dreams these contents speak to us in a language whose images have been present in the souls of men from time immemorial.[99]

One and four

In Chinese symbolism the square is identified with the earth; in that of India with the *padma* (lotus) or *mandala* (protected, sacred precinct). In both cases it has the character of the Yoni, the feminine, the "container."[100] Construed as earth, it was viewed in Christian mysticism as the matrix, so to speak, the native soil of the divine, as the "Mater Dei," the Theotokos.[101] Hence it is by no means surprising that in our dream the "blue mists" in their quadratic arrangement should form the psychic space within which the "One," the pre-existent image of God dwelling in the psyche, is born and takes form. God, *"der liebe Gott,"* as the dreamer calls him in her childlike faith, appears in his omnipotence to defeat the monster of darkness. Thus far the dream has been on two planes: the animal-material, to which the "Bad Animal" belongs, and

[98] "Psychology and Religion," par. 100.

[99] Thus when Jung, in order to amplify and interpret this language, draws on past conceptions and their symbols (e.g., those of the various mythologies or of Gnosticism), he only wishes to demonstrate that these ancient ideas and symbols are still alive in the material that rises from the unconscious of modern man and not—as has often been suggested by his critics—to profess his faith in Gnosticism as a religion or philosophy.

[100] *Psychology and Alchemy*, p. 143.

[101] "Psychology and Religion," par. 107.

the intermediary realm of the psyche, represented by the "blue fog." Now, with the appearance of God, the third plane is introduced, that of the spiritual and divine as supreme fulfillment. In the dramatic course of the dream all three become actualized and operative.

"The quaternity," says Jung, "is a more or less direct representation of the God who is manifest in his creation."[102] As a dream symbol it points to the "God within," and the archetypal images with which the psyche lends expression to this inner God bear witness to its divine nature. The soul appears as a vessel for the spirit whose dwelling place (similar to the divine spark dwelling in the square of the *temenos*) is in the four-times-enclosed precinct of its "inner sanctuary." One is reminded of Buddha enthroned in the middle of the lotus, the eternal birthplace of the gods.[103]

Fundamentally all squareness strives toward a midpoint. For the Four achieves its ultimate fulfillment only in the manifestation of the One.[104] This "One" as a summation of the quaternity has left its deposit in numerous images and figures of speech and led to far-reaching speculations. It is a widespread archetypal motif. It is also known to us as the *quinta essentia*, which represents a kind of synthesis or concentration of all the powers represented in the four. As early a writer as Plutarch noted: "For the

[102] Ibid., par. 101.
[103] The square pattern in Mohammedan prayer mats symbolizes the dwelling place of the believer, who, as one partaking in him, takes the place of God himself.
[104] The Coptic philosopher Maria Prophetissa (known in alchemical literature as Mary the Jewess) is quoted as saying: "One becomes Two, Two becomes Three, and out of the Third comes the One as the Fourth." These mysterious words embody the entire meaning set forth above: the gathering of the four into a unity. (Cf. *Psychology and Alchemy*, p. 23.)

beginning of all number is one, and the first square is four; and from these, as though from perfected form and matter, comes five."[105] In alchemy the "One" is the "quintessence," the result of the process whose purpose it is to produce it, to extract it from the four elements. The mathematical riddle of the "squaring of the circle," which busied so many philosophical minds for centuries, represents the mystical union of the four elements. ". . . The point in the center, the *quinta essentia*, is the mediator, or, expressed in alchemical language, the *pelicanus noster* (our Pelican). Of this mediator it is said that it is he who brings about the squaring of the circle, and who therefore symbolizes the secret and at the same time its solution."[106]

The five, or in other words the quaternity united in the quintessence, is not a derivative, however, but an independent whole that is more than the sum of its parts. It is the superessential that transcends all the rest. The throne of God borne by the four cherubim with the four faces in Ezekiel's vision,[107] the triumphant Saviour amid the four symbolic figures of the Evangelists, the Tibetan deity Vairochana, the omnipresent, the father-mother unity who is always seated in the center of the mandala,[108] are impressive examples of this.

The Yogi strives for a "consciousness in four aspects" in order to penetrate to the "One," the highest spiritual stage uniting all others, and thereby to attain to the state of "Buddha consciousness," "the illuminating diamond essence."[109] This is somewhat analogous to the strange

105 Plutarch, "The E at Delphi," in *Moralia*, V, 233.
106 ETH Lectures, 1938/39, p. 115. [Here tr. R.F.C.H.]
107 Ezekiel 1 : 6-7, 26.
108 Evans-Wentz, *The Tibetan Book of the Dead*, p. 119.
109 ETH Lectures, 1938/39, p. 55.

happening of our dream, related in the childlike words: "And then God came, but there were really four Gods in the four corners." How simple it sounds, and yet what meaning and tension, what moving grandeur there is behind the words!

As we have seen, the quaternity of the "blue mists" was the harbinger of the One "God," forming at the same time the "psychic square" out of which he emerges from invisibility into full visibility. Another aspect of fourness, namely the four-sided unfolding of the One, is made manifest in the second quaternity, that of the "four Gods." It is as though the One were sending forth the four, so that the self-limited unity should be able to radiate without limit in all four directions. Here the four symbolize the parts, qualities, and aspects of the One.[110] For the One is the primordial beginning, but it is also the summation of all possibilities and developments and therefore symbolizes both the beginning and the end. Thus there is a kind of identity and reciprocal relation between the One and the *quinta essentia*.

The dream does not tell us whether the One "God" vanishes when the "four Gods" appear or remains present along with them, as their quintessence, so to speak. In the latter case we might cite the Chinese analogy of *Ch'ien* (Heaven), with its four radiating cosmic powers, or the Mohammedan face of God which according to the Koran looks from all four directions upon the actions of the faithful, or the Buddhist God Vajra whose four heads are turned toward the four cardinal points (he is said to have been split into four parts, but was welded together again into a unity, in which, however, the four parts are still

[110] "Psychology and Religion," par. 98.

visible).[111] The separation of the One into the four is a process of differentiation which enhances the powers of the One and enables it to extend to all four horizons. In the sphere of psychic development a similar pattern underlies the stabilization, broadening, and maturation of the ego, which is accompanied by the progressive differentiation of the four functions of consciousness (thinking, feeling, intuition, sensation).

But it is unimportant for our interpretation whether we have here a single God who subsequently manifests himself in a fourfold form, or whether he is replaced by the "four Gods" (i.e., whether we have a simultaneity or a succession, a One plus four or a quaternity grown out of the One, or for that matter a theophany in which the "four Gods" alone dominate the dream stage). The four, the One, the five are protagonists in a widely distributed number symbolism which brings out the fullness of meaning contained in our dream. And because throughout the history of symbols four has been regarded as "feminine" and one or five as "masculine," we may perhaps discern here, in the world of the "upper process," the immanent opposition that we have already seen in the realm of the "lower process," that is to say, in the male-female polarity of the "Bad Animal."

We may observe that, both in the traditional Eastern mandalas and in the individual modern mandalas of the West, one half reflects the dark "lower world" and the other the bright "upper world." The cross is erected between hell and heaven, its two beams extending in all four directions. Similarly in this simple childhood dream, we behold a magnificent image of the cosmic quaternity

[111] ETH Lectures, 1938/39, p. 114.

formed by the two pairs of opposites inherent in the "lower" and "upper" processes.[112] Born from the depths of the unconscious psyche, the dream bears witness to an unconscious knowledge of man's participation in both worlds, the mortal and the immortal, and to the painful antinomy of his being that clings to both.[113]

In its supreme magnificence and glory the fourfold godhead represents the climax of the dream. It brings about

[112] An attempt to represent the pairs of opposites in a diagram might yield the following sketch:

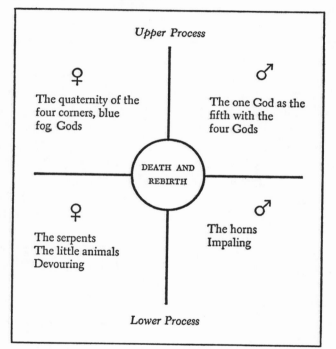

[113] "The Cross is imprinted upon man, even upon his face," says Justin Martyr (*Apology*, I, 55); it is the symbol of "man in his contradiction."

the triumphant end. All the darkness and evil of the "lower process" are replaced by the liberating power of the "upper process." The ultimate authority, the all-powerful and loving God, turns the wheel, and a new beginning is inaugurated.

The rebirth

We are approaching the end, the lysis of the dream: "Then the animal died and all the animals it had eaten came out alive again." The circle is closed, the dead have arisen. The "little animals" have not met their doom inside the dragon's body, they have only experienced a kind of journey to hell, a state of containment in the darkness, and have awakened to new life. "And I saw an angel come down from heaven. . . . And he laid hold on the dragon, that old serpent, which is the Devil, and Satan. . . . And cast him into the bottomless pit. . . . And I saw a new heaven and a new earth."[114] So the Apocalypse. And here too a heavenly power, "God" himself, has appeared; though he has not cast the "Bad Animal" into the bottomless pit, he has put an end to its voracity and brought about its death, so that the vital substances it has destroyed, the "little animals," can be born again. Whether this requires an "act" on his part, or whether his mere appearance suffices, we do not know. For the child's psyche, God reveals his power by "love"; her faith in his "love" is still unshaken and unlimited.

The idea of rebirth, renewal, conquest of death is far from being an exclusively Christian heritage. It has flourished among all peoples and in all cultures. "Rebirth is

[114] Revelation 20 : 1-3; 21 : 1.

an affirmation that must be counted among the primordial affirmations of mankind,"[115] says Jung. As such it rests on an archetypal ground pattern which underlies the psychic process and its expression in myth and rite. The mystery of rebirth, for fundamentally that is what we are dealing with in this dream, can be represented in innumerable forms and aspects.[116] In his illuminating work "Concerning Rebirth"[117] Jung takes up some of the most important.

One of these forms, the motif of the "hatching out of the universe," preserved in an endless series of myths and legends, represents as it were the rebirth of a whole "world" and not only that of a single "creature." The various traditions of a deluge, sometimes symbolized as a devouring water monster, and of a new world built by those saved, are another example.[118] The conclusion of our dream points in this direction.

Every rebirth is preceded by a "death." This "death" can occur on all levels and in all domains of life and can be expressed in symbols. The ensuing rebirth assumes every conceivable form from a *restitutio ad integrum* of the former mode of existence, to an utterly changed new manifestation. At the beginning of history the daily reappearance of the sun from out of the "sea dragon" and other similar natural processes no doubt constituted the basis of the rebirth symbolism; but in the course of time

[115] "Concerning Rebirth" (C. W. 9, i), par. 207.

[116] Ibid., secs. 1-2.

[117] Many outstanding ethnologists and historians of religion have collected an abundance of material on this theme. Here I can mention only a very few of the works relevant to our discussion: Gunkel, *Schöpfung und Chaos in Urzeit und Endzeit* (1895); Frobenius, *Das Zeitalter des Sonnengottes* (1904); Mircea Eliade, *The Myth of the Eternal Return* (tr., 1955); and Hentze, *Tod, Auferstehung, Weltordnung* (1955).

[118] See n. 117, foregoing.

the idea of transformation assumed an increasingly prominent place, side by side with that of resurrection. Apocatastasis on the purely natural plane of being is a mere restoration of the original state, but in the domain of the psyche it can represent a "resurrection" on a "higher plane," an improvement, ennoblement, transfiguration, etc. The pain and torment of death stand symbolically for the sacrifice that must always be made before the new can come into being: "And the Lord spake unto the fish, and it vomited out Jonah upon the dry land."[119] But the Biblical narrative does not tell us what became of the whale or whether Jonah was "changed" after his "rebirth." On the other hand, the hero in the whale-dragon myth related by Frobenius[120] loses his hair in the fire of the monster's body; he has to make a "sacrifice," i.e., he not only goes through suffering but loses his hair, symbol of the power of thought, and comes forth changed, matured.[121]

The higher the level of consciousness of the individual in whom the transformation occurs (as the alchemists and mystics in particular believed) and the farther removed it is from the purely cyclical course of nature, the more the final state will differ from the initial state and the closer it will come to the imperishable and indestructible. This explains the countless rites of initiation even among primitive peoples, the Yogis' strivings for spiritual illumination, and the quest of the mystics of all religions for inward enlightenment. All these strivings were held to help man attain to essential insights through struggle, suffering, and inner meditation, and so achieve a symbolic rebirth on a "higher level." The conception of a first, mortal Adam who

[119] Jonah 2: 10. Cf. also Frobenius, *Das Zeitalter des Sonnengottes*, p. 66. Cf. also our fig. 4.
[120] Cf. below, p. 180.
[121] See Frobenius, p. 62, and diagram on our p. 181.

is redeemed and becomes a second, purified, immortal Adam[122] runs like a red thread through the thought of Christianity, Gnosticism, and alchemy.

Basically every transition, from one phase of life to another, from sleeping to waking, from unconsciousness to conscious knowledge, etc., signifies a kind of "rebirth." And every new insight in life is accompanied by a transformation in which something superseded must die, must be left behind. Every "transformation" is actually a mystery and as such an integral part of life. And in the conceptions regarding "rebirth"—regardless of whether they relate to a single rebirth or to a chain of rebirths—transformation is ultimately bound up with the mystery of life itself.[123]

Have the "little animals" changed in the belly of the "Bad Animal," or are they reborn the same as they were at the time of their death? The dream gives no answer. Still, there has been a fundamental change: the "Bad Animal" has died, the darkness that it symbolized is overcome, replaced by the luminous world of the divine. A new "creation" has begun; the destructive activity of the beast of chaos is ended.[124]

This means, in psychological language, that the dangerous, aggressive, destructive activity of the primordial

[122] See also p. 167, above.

[123] According to Herbert Silberer, two fundamental principles are common to the various interpretations of the rites of rebirth: 1) a radical upheaval in life or elevation to a new, more perfect mode of life; 2) a relation to the mysterious powers of the beyond, the divine (*Durch Tod zum Leben*, pp. 50 ff.).

[124] For Mircea Eliade, for example, "every New Year [is] the inauguration of an era," an "eternal repetition of the cosmogonic act," and so likewise every renewal is at the same time a new act of creation, a "new birth." (*The Myth of the Eternal Return*, pp. 62 f.)

depths of the unconscious, expressed by the impaling and devouring of the intrapsychic substances and components, the "little animals," has been made ineffectual and eliminated by the appearance of a contrary power, i.e., the manifestation of the divine. The fourfold godhead as the archetypal representative of a supreme, ordering, and fate-like authority dwelling within the psyche, namely, the self, has interceded and transformed "chaos into a cosmos."

The night sea journey

It is not only the meaning of the dream elements, of the archetypal motifs contained in it, that can be elucidated by the use of amplificatory material. The entire dream action, which as a whole discloses a basic archetypal ground pattern, can be subjected to the same interpretive method. A whole series of myths, sagas, and fairytales can be drawn in as parallels, among them a number of creation myths, to which the dream shows many analogies. But the closest correspondence is provided by the initiation rites, the mysteries of renewal or rebirth[125] based on the model of the "night sea journey,"[126] the so-called "Nekyia,"[127] in all their forms. Life, death, and rebirth in their interpenetration form the three great dramatic segments of a process that embraces and underlies them all.

According to Frobenius, who in his book *Das Zeitalter des Sonnengottes* ("The Age of the Sun God") collected from all over the world a large number of myths of this type, to which he gave the name "whale-dragon myth,"

[125] Cf. p. 76 and p. 103, above.

[126] The nocturnal "journey of the sun," or of the solar hero through the sea, the underworld, etc.

[127] The journey to Hades, the descent into the land of the dead (subject of the eleventh book of the Odyssey).

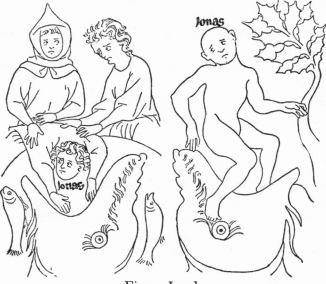

Fig. 3. Jonah

Left: He is thrown into the sea and devoured by the whale. Right:
He is disgorged, bald and naked, the ivy branch he grasps in his left
hand symbolizing the earth (solid ground) regained. Drawings from
a 14th-cent. ms. of the "Biblia pauperum."

all have the following characteristic schematic course,
which occurs in innumerable variations:

"A hero is devoured by a water monster in the West
(*swallowing*). The animal travels with him to the East
(*sea journey*). Meanwhile, the hero lights a fire in the
belly of the monster (*fire-lighting*), and feeling hungry,
cuts himself a piece of the heart (*cutting off of heart*).
Soon afterwards he notices that the fish has glided to dry
land (*landing*); he immediately begins to cut open the
animal from within (*opening*); then he slips out (*slipping
out*). It was so hot in the fish's belly that all his hair has

fallen out (*heat and hair*). The hero may at the same time free all of those who were previously devoured by the monster."[128]

Here is the sketch provided by Frobenius, slightly adapted to our purpose:

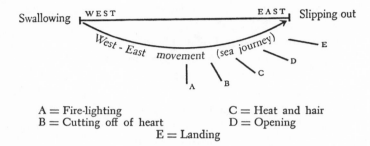

A = Fire-lighting   C = Heat and hair
B = Cutting off of heart   D = Opening
          E = Landing

Even though all the elements and features of this paradigm do not occur in our dream, one cannot but find a surprising analogy. In most of these myths it is human beings who are devoured and reborn and not "little animals" as in our dream, but this makes no essential difference, for the little animals, if taken as "soul substances," present an analogy to the myths cited by Frobenius, in which the whale devours the "souls" of men, carries them into the beyond, and there spews them forth,[129] or the stars in the form of "kids"—again animals—are swallowed up by the wolf, symbol of the dark night, the unconscious. Frobenius mentions different variants of the whale-dragon myth, of which the so-called "animalistic-solar" type comes closest to our dream. In myths, according to Frobenius, man, the hero, woman, etc., stand for anthropo-

[128] Frobenius, p. 421; as quoted in *Symbols of Transformation*, par. 310.
[129] Frobenius, pp. 197 and 219.

morphically conceived heavenly bodies (chiefly the sun), hence in a certain sense psychologically for consciousness, and specifically the adult consciousness. But here we have the dream of a child whose consciousness is not yet crystallized out, and in whom the "soul substances" might very well represent those elements from whose subsequent differentiation will issue, after their "rebirth," the future, stabilized consciousness of the adult.

In the myth of the Great Thornback found by Frobenius among the Oyster Bay tribe in Tasmania,[130] the analogy is even plainer. This Thornback was said to lie in a cave and to have a long spear with which he pierced the women whom he spied through the hole in his cave as they dived into the water. He killed them with his spear and carried them away. For a time they were not to be seen. Then the hero came, defeated the monster, lighted a fire, and brought the women back to life. Here we find almost all the elements of our dream: the bad horned animal = the Thornback with his spear; the little animals = the women who are impaled and vanish; the appearance of God and the four Gods = the rescue by the hero; the rebirth of the little animals = the resuscitation of the women.[131]

And who does not know the tale—to mention only one of many with the same import—of Little Red Riding Hood, who along with her grandmother is devoured by the wicked wolf and after his death comes forth alive? Does it not convey a related meaning?

As models of a creation myth, we may mention the Babylonian myth of Marduk and Tiamat, and the Egyp-

[130] *Symbols of Transformation* contains numerous myths of similar content and much additional material on the present theme.
[131] Frobenius, p. 77.

tian myth of Osiris, Horus, and Set. In both myths there
was universal water in the beginning. Both myths per-
sonify this universal water as an evil monster or dragon;[132]
both end with the victory of the solar hero—Marduk or
Horus. Marduk fights the typical battle of the solar hero
with the dragon, the hungry maw of hell, in which men are
engulfed just as. the "little animals" of the dream are
devoured by the "Bad Animal." In mythical terms many
cosmogonies are a conquest of the Great Mother, the terrible monster, by a hero, conceived as a victory of the order-
bringing light over the chaotic "preconfigurational modal-
ity of the universe,"[133] which thereby takes form.

From the standpoint of the individual psyche, entry
into the belly of a monster is equivalent to the submer-
sion of consciousness in the unconscious, the return to the
womb. This "return," however, is not entirely negative, not just a "regression." It is—according to Jung—
a necessary occurrence that should be evaluated positively.
For the unconscious is not only the maw of death; it contains also all those nourishing and creative energies that
are at the root of life. When contact is made with them,
they are revived and put at the disposal of consciousness;
they are "reborn." The contents of our consciousness experience a "night sea journey," like the "little animals" in
our dream, and like Osiris, the sun god who enters into
the womb, into the coffer, the sea, the tree, and who then,
dismembered, re-formed and reborn, reappears in his son.[134]
This insight supports Jung's prospective view of regression;
it is based on his psychotherapeutic experience, which

[132] The serpent Apophis, symbolizing the primordial water; Set,
who was sometimes represented as a crocodile; and Tiamat, who
was said to be a "furious serpent."
[133] Eliade, p. 40, n. 70 (mod.).
[134] *Symbols of Transformation*, p. 242.

finds parallels and corroboration in an abundance of myths.

The hero must, as it were, be enclosed in the mother as a preparation for rebirth. Thus Heracles undertakes his nocturnal journey in a golden bowl,[135] and Noah, borne by his ark, reaches the new morning with all that remains of the old world. Another such "vessel" is the goddess Nut of Egyptian mythology: daily she swallows up the sun and daily rebears him from her womb.[136]

The symbolic identity between sun, hero, and man[137]— as it appears in the archetypal sequence of the "night sea journey"—is charmingly expressed in a profoundly meaningful Chinese rite. At the time of the Han Dynasty it was customary in China to make coffins out of four boards, taken from four different trees growing in the four regions. The drapery over the coffin was colored according to the four points of heaven and the four sides of the coffin were adorned with the four animals symbolizing the four quarters of heaven. At the top the drapery was drawn together in a pyramid whose tip symbolized the North Pole, and the seven stars of the Great Bear were distributed over the coffin. The entire arrangement was known as the *great dragon*, the chariot in which the sun journeyed over the heavenly ocean at night. Since a correspondence was seen between a man's death and the setting of the sun, the corpse was placed in the coffin at the time of the rains when the sun is devoured by the water, and it was taken as a sign of future happiness if abundant rain fell when the grave was closed. But the most important con-

[135] Kerényi, *Töchter der Sonne* (1944), p. 28, fig. 2. (In this connection heroes such as Heracles are often identified with the sun.) Cf. *Symbols of Transformation*, p. 205.
[136] E. A. Wallis Budge, *The Gods of the Egyptians* (1904), II, 101. See also *Symbols of Transformation*, p. 241, fig. 24.
[137] Cf. pp. 46 f., above.

sideration was the place where the coffin was lowered, for if rebirth was to be assured, it had to be a "place of the middle," where all four zones of the world and their energies could achieve equal unfolding.[138] This custom speaks for itself. We even discover in it the same great importance which is attached to the quaternity in our dream, and if we reduce the ritual to its essentials, they will be found to correspond quite closely to those of our "night sea journey."

The setting and rising of the sun as entry into the womb and eternally recurrent rebirth (which in the psychic domain may be defined as a waning and revival of psychic energy) is also an image of time and its course, which the alchemists symbolized by the uroboros—again a dragon.[139] The snake or dragon biting its tail in token of eternal rebirth symbolized the *opus circulare* of alchemy,[140] the course of all life, the wheel of Samsara, the eternal cycle.

But in the myths and fairytales time is not always related to the course of the sun; the segments are often determined by the phases of the moon. A delightful example of this is the fairytale of the wolf and the seven young kids.[141] After a number of crafty attempts the wolf, i.e., night, succeeds in eating the kids, the phases of the moon, but in the end, while the wolf is asleep—i.e., while the sky is moonless—the mother goat cuts open his belly and all come forth in good health, so that the moon

[138] Fuhrmann, *Das Tier in der Religion*, p. 29.

[139] Cf. *Psychology and Alchemy*, p. 45, fig. 6.

[140] "Nature rejoices in nature, nature subdues nature, nature rules over nature," says a late anonymous Latin author, Pseudo-Democritus, referring to the *opus circulare* of alchemy, symbolized by the uroboros. (As quoted in "Psychology of the Transference," C. W. 16, p. 261, n. 10.)

[141] *Grimm's Fairy Tales*, no. 5.

185

can begin to grow again. But regardless of whether we have a solar or lunar symbolism, the significant factor is the structural similarity, the cyclical process, the continuity of the chain of rebirths. In this connection the "little animals" may represent the time segments that make up the cycle (cf. fig. 3).

But seen from another standpoint, the night sea journey may be taken as a unique and decisive experience in which the accent is not on the "eternal recurrence" of the same thing, but on a "transformation into something higher." The "little animals" would then be the *prima materia* that is in need of transformation and the whole dream a kind of individual, or cosmic, mystery of redemption. Whether the meaning of the dream is more compatible with a Christian conception, which recognizes only one redemption of the world and man, or with a pagan-mythological conception which—like the Indian or Germanic—looks on creation, death, and rebirth as a recurrent cycle, depends on the standpoint of the observer.

Jung draws an analogy between the "way of individuation" and the archetypal image of the night sea journey.[142] Once the psyche reaches the midpoint of life, the process of development demands a return to the beginning, a descent into the dark, hot depths of the unconscious. To sojourn in these depths, to withstand their dangers, is a journey to hell and "death." But he who comes through safe and sound, who is "reborn," will return, full of knowledge and wisdom, equipped for the outward and inward demands of life. He has pressed forward to his limits and has taken his destiny upon himself. This "great Nekyia," which usually leads to the very threshold

[142] See pp. 113 f., above.

of the beyond, is interwoven with innumerable lesser Nekyia experiences, all the many psychic sufferings, upheavals, darknesses, that run through every life. To endure and withstand these experiences helps the individual to greater insight and security. The great arc of the night sea journey comprises many lesser rhythms, lesser arcs on the same "primordial pattern." Here again there is a close connection between the unique event and cyclic recurrence.

To this event, whose meaning remains essentially the same, mankind has given ever new forms, which rise up from the depths of the psyche in the variegated richness of eternally renewed archetypal images. Birth, life, death, and rebirth belong together; they are a totality; they represent a "primordial pattern" which finds its expression in symbols either reflecting it as a rounded unity or disclosing it as separate links in an endless chain, as "a moment of eternity in time."[143]

The content of an archetypal image is always overdetermined; it can be interpreted and understood on different levels; seen in several aspects, it preserves the same meaning. The "night sea journey," as a unique event or as a link in a chain of many repetitions, has even left its deposit in the myths. There are whale-dragon myths in which the dragon spews out what it has swallowed, then goes on living, devours new victims, and vomits them up again, etc.; and others in which the victims are reborn but the dragon meets its death—as in our dream.

Does the dream of the "Bad Animal," taken as a paradigm, represent a single "link" in a chain of recurrent dramas, or a unique drama? If we take the dream for itself, as a kind of model for the archetype of the "night

[143] "Concerning Rebirth" (C. W. 9, i), par. 209.

sea journey," without regard to the dreamer, both interpretations are possible. But if we take the dreamer into consideration—and without doing so it is impossible to do justice to the dream—we should not overlook the fact that the scene of the great conflict between the two worlds of the animal and the divine is the unconscious psyche of the little girl herself, and that all our analogies are merely a metaphorical expression of this event. For the little girl the dream and what it had to communicate were a single, unrepeated occurrence, but the "night sea journey" of her soul substances, of the "little animals," was at the same time an experience in which the components of an individual psyche merged with the archetypal images of the collective source, to partake of rebirth.

Thus in one respect the dream is a segment in an endless and timeless process of dying and becoming, but in another it is a unique, self-contained occurrence. In each of these segments the torment of death and the triumph of resurgent life are repeated, forming a parallel to what every individual experiences uniquely and unrepeatably, but at the same time they are a link within the chain of the generations, in the endless series of the human species. In this sense the personal and unique, the collective and typical, are so close together as to be almost indistinguishable. "At bottom," says Jung, "all psychic events are so deeply grounded in the archetype and are so much interwoven with it that in every case considerable critical effort is needed to separate the unique from the typical with certainty. Ultimately, every individual life is at the same time the eternal life of the species."[144] Understood in this way, the dream reveals both the eternally

[144] "Psychology and Religion" (C. W. 11), par. 146.

renewed, unchanging course of nature, and the potential victory of spirit over matter, which must forever be gained anew if life is to acquire a profounder meaning. This applies as much to the individual life as to the endless chain of all creatures. For not only does the individual stand in the middle of the cosmos; the cosmos is also in ourselves.

"I can only stop and gaze with admiration and awe," writes Jung, "at the depths and heights of our psychic nature. Its nonspatial world conceals an untold abundance of images that have been amassed and organically consolidated during millions of years of development. My consciousness is like an eye that contains in itself the most distant spaces, yet it is the psychic nonego that fills them nonspatially. And these images are not pale shadows, but tremendously powerful psychic factors. The most we may be able to do is to misunderstand them, but we can never rob them of their power by denying them. Beside this picture I would like to place that of the starry vistas of the heavens at night, for the only equivalent of the world within is the world without, and just as I reach this world through the medium of the body, so I reach that world through the medium of the psyche."[145]

[145] Jung's Introduction to Otto Kranefeldt, *Secret Ways of the Mind* (1932), p. xxxix. [C. W., final vol. Here revised by R.F.C.H.]

CONCLUSION

In the "Dream of the Bad Animal,"[1] the dreamer is confronted with an inner reality that far exceeds her powers of understanding; this reality, which can only disclose itself in symbols, bears witness to the mysterious power of the unconscious psyche. The dreamer herself experiences the dream, but her conscious ego stands outside it. She remembers the dream, but makes no comment on it. Nor can our powers of interpretation ever encompass all the richness of meaning concealed in such a dream. Its amazing succinctness and completeness, its unfathomable depth will forever evade full interpretation and adequate expression. What little we are able to note here is only a modest attempt to contribute to its better understanding.

*   *

If we bear in mind that dreams—in Jung's view—are a self-representation of events in the unconscious and a compensation for the situation of the conscious mind, we must attempt to understand this dream as relating to a particular situation in life. It is difficult to draw inferences regarding this situation as reflected in the dreamer's outward life, because the dream contains no personal associations and because neither the outward nor the inward circumstances attending it are available to us. But we do know that when such clearly archetypal and symbolic dreams appear, it is always in existentially significant constellations. "It is very probable," says Jung, "that the

[1] Cf. pp. 139 ff., above.

190

activation of an archetype depends on an alteration of the conscious situation, which requires a new form of compensation."[2] In investigating the meaning of such dreams, we can approach them only from very general standpoints and on the basis of our experience in dealing with such material.

In this dream one is particularly struck by the indistinct and rather blurred character of the various dream elements—the Bad Animal, the little animals, the blue fog, God, and the four Gods. It suggests that these are collective archetypal images which have remained very largely untouched by individual experience, i.e., which belong to a very deep "stratum" of the psyche. For it has often been observed that the more a problem is conditioned by temporal and personal factors, the more intricate, detailed, and sharp will be the image or dream in which it is expressed. The more universal and impersonal the problem, the more symbolic and sparse will be the manner of expression. Detailed, sharply outlined dreams relate as a rule to purely personal problems and usually spring from the realm of the personal unconscious. Those presenting sparse details and simple images afford insights into the great problems of the world and life[3] and, as in this case, arise from the collective unconscious. They always indicate the dreamer's profound immersion in it.

This is by no means unusual in children, for their ego is not yet consolidated and is closer than that of adults to the collective sources of the psyche. Nevertheless, a dream possessing such cosmic symbolism and such a dynamic charge occurs but seldom and reflects, in archetypal

[2] "A Psychological Approach to the Dogma of the Trinity" (C. W. 11), par. 223, n. 4.

[3] See pp. 107 f., above.

images and happenings, a profoundly disturbing actual conflict which presumably the conscious mind cannot understand or resolve.

We know that the dreamer was eight years old and relatively advanced in her development, that she may already have been in the first phase of prepuberty. At such times the unconscious is always subject to a particular restlessness and mobility, which is often manifested in dreams of great creative power. The future is still hidden in the unconscious and can present itself to us only in the form of symbols. We also know that the dreamer died a year later; although the infectious disease that caused her death cannot have set in at the time of the dream, the child's psyche may already have had a premonition of it. Jung says expressly: "However incomprehensible it may appear, we are finally compelled to assume that there is in the unconscious something like an *a priori* knowledge or an 'immediacy' of events which lacks any causal basis." This knowledge may manifest itself in dreams in the form of archetypal images that "stand in a . . . meaningful relationship to objective occurrences which have no recognizable or even conceivable causal relationship with them."[4] And elsewhere: "I have had occasion to observe . . . that in certain cases of longstanding neurosis a dream, often of visionary clarity, occurs about the time of the onset of the illness *or shortly before,*[5] which imprints itself indelibly on the mind and, when analyzed, reveals to the patient a hidden meaning that anticipates the subsequent events of his life."[6] These events may not occur until several months later.[7] As the inner

---

[4] "Synchronicity," par. 856.   [5] Italics mine.—J.J.
[6] *Symbols of Transformation,* pp. 50-51.
[7] This is equally true when a dream of this type occurs **without**

eye beholds the archetypal images in a dream, it may discern the predestined end.[8] For space and time are categories that spring from consciousness, from its "discriminating activity." The time that prevails in the collective unconscious and its manifestations is the "mythical time" in which past and future are one, that is to say, always the present.[9]

According to Jung, the "natural processes of transformation," which are innate in all living beings and play so large a role in the period of puberty, underlie all ideas of rebirth; they "announce themselves mainly in dreams."[10] They come upon us whether we like it or not. And because every "transition" from one phase to another leads through the "death" of the old to the "birth" of the new, dreams containing rebirth symbolism point to a lesser or greater crisis in the dreamer, a conclusion that is confirmed by observation. Hence it is quite conceivable that the psychic situation of our little dreamer was one of tension or even of danger[11] at the time when the dream occurred.

Another indication of this is that she seems to have lived in particularly close contact with the world of inner images, for otherwise she would scarcely have conceived

---

analysis; then its meaning remains hidden from the dreamer but is confirmed in the subsequent events of his life.

[8] "Everything old in our unconscious hints at something coming," says Jung. *Psychological Types,* p. 549. [Tr. here by R.F.C.H.]

[9] Borrowing from St. Augustine, Jung expresses this in the apt words: "What happens successively in time is simultaneous in the mind of God." ("Synchronicity," par. 967, n. 17.)

[10] "Concerning Rebirth," pars. 234f.

[11] "Experience shows that individual mandalas are symbols of *order* and that they occur in patients chiefly during times of psychic disorientation or reorientation. As magic circles they bind and subdue the lawless powers belonging to the world of darkness, and depict or create an order that transforms the chaos into a cosmos." *Aion,* par. 60.

the idea, surely unusual for a child of her age, of giving her father her dreams as a Christmas present. She must have attached great importance to them, taken them seriously. The dream of the "Bad Animal" was the last of this series. In it the central problem of the immanent bipolarity of the psyche is raised and the bestial-divine, dual nature of man, the tension of opposites in the self, is dramatically enacted.[12] Thus our dream may be a kind of summary or even an attempt to give a final meaning to the preceding series of dreams.

The godhead has triumphed; the world of light seems secured, for the monster is dead and the reborn "little animals" can develop in unthreatened freedom. The falling away of the dark world may at first have given a soothing feeling of safety, a sense of salvation. By way of compensation, it gave the dreamer's psyche the faith and security which she probably lacked in her waking life. Particularly in sheltered and sensitive children (and the little dreamer was surely one of these), the anxieties of the day, which they scarcely admit to themselves, often obtain an answer and appeasement in dreams.[13] An indefinable anxiety is a frequent symptom in children. Fear of life and fear of death lie close together, scarcely differentiated, in the child's mind. Children live in a world of all-powerful giants, the grownups, and have difficulty in

[12] Concerning the self and its immanent antinomy, the reader is referred to Jung's writings, particularly *Psychology and Alchemy* and *Aion*, and his two volumes on the *Mysterium Coniunctionis*.

[13] In an interesting article, "Die anankastische Selbstregulation in Lebenskrisen" (1954), R. Bilz, of the Mainz Psychiatrische Nervenklinik, writes: "There is an inner iatros [physician], a psychotherapist in the child . . . an endogenous regenerator of balance which brings about the *restitutio ad integrum*. . . . Indeed it is our conviction that there is an agency of self-healing which makes use of playful, cathartic means, and dreams seem to subserve these health-restoring mechanisms."

orienting themselves in the struggle between good and evil. However, the loss of the underworld, of the dark counterpart of the luminous gods, can only be temporary in this earthly life, in dreams or fantasies, for example. Otherwise, the soul of the dreamer would enter immediately into a perpetually bright world, into "heaven," and be lost to earthly reality. It is in the nature of the human being that the two powers should combat one another in the depths of the soul, and this perpetual conflict is a part of the paradox of all life.

States of excitation in the prepubertal period, real conflicts with the environment and fears of the dark element in it, the struggle between good and evil, reaching down to the bottommost depths of the soul—these conflicts, all calling for a "higher intervention" that would eliminate or solve them, as well as an unconscious intimation of her imminent death, may have contributed to the making of this dream. But let us set aside the usual reductive formulations of the problem, the "Whence?" and "Why?" and in the spirit of Jung's analytical psychology, and mindful of the purposive character of psychic processes, ask "To what end?" To what end was just this dream dreamed in this form, with this content, and at this time?

This question brings us to a new consideration, which cannot be dismissed out of hand, and which may give us an orienting hint. Like participation in mysteries and initiations, rites and cults, or attendance at great dramatic works, a dream—and particularly a dream of great expressive power—can leave behind it the certainty of an immediate and concrete experience, as though the experience had befallen the dreamer in a waking state. It imprints itself on the psyche from within and goes on working in it, even if it is accompanied by no outward event, and this usually with no conscious participation of the ego. One who has partaken of the mystery of death and rebirth in a dream—such as that of the "Bad Animal"—may well learn in his heart that the end can at the same time be a beginning. He may learn that it is possible—if only in the likeness of a dream—to suffer death and yet not to die, to return alive from the body of the beast of chaos, from the dark night of the underworld, and this will always be a unique and powerful experience. A faint intimation of immortality may thus arise in the soul and help to settle its storms.

Birth, life, death, and rebirth are four elements of the same mystery, and between them there is no cleavage. But if there is no cleavage, all fear of death vanishes. In this light, we may perhaps be justified in taking the dream as an "attempt" on the part of the unconscious to impart to the little dreamer the primordial cosmic image, and at the same time its reflection in the human psyche of the way that leads through death to new life.

Is this, perhaps, the "truth" that the dream wished to communicate to the little girl? Was it given to her as a guide along the way, a consoling prospect, a helpful revelation? Who would venture to decide?

*　　*

"A dream never says 'You ought' or 'This is the truth.' It presents an image in much the same way as nature allows a plant to grow, and we must draw our own conclusions. . . . To grasp its meaning, we must allow it to shape us. . . . Then we understand the nature of the experience. We see that the dreamer has drawn upon the healing and redeeming forces of the collective psyche that underlies consciousness with its isolation and its painful errors; he has penetrated to that matrix of life in which all men are embedded, which imparts a common rhythm to all human existence, and allows the individual to communicate his feeling and his striving to mankind as a whole."[14] The return to the state of *participation mystique* is the secret which the experience of a dream vouchsafes us; and to sink ourselves in its archetypal images, to become one with them, can have a transforming and healing effect on the soul of the dreamer.

Fig. 4. Uroboros

One of the earliest symbols of the alchemists: the serpent biting its own tail. In Egypt, it represented the circle of the Universe or the path of the sun god. The Greek inscription ἓν τὸ πᾶν (all is one) is often found in the center of the uroboric circle. To the alchemist the uroboros symbolized the mysterious circulation of chemical substances in the hermetic vessel during distillation. Drawing from a Greek ms. of the Alexandrian period, containing the "Chrysopoeia" (Gold-making), a work attributed to the woman alchemist "Cleopatra."

Every dream is a statement of the psyche about itself. That the psyche should thus reveal itself to a child shortly before her death, in this profound way, is an amazing fact—one might call it the miracle of the helpful col-

[14] "Psychology and Literature," in *Modern Man in Search of a Soul*, p. 198. [C. W. 15.]

laboration of the unconscious. The answer to the secrets of the day and the solutions to the riddles of the future are all contained in its primordial womb. That is why there is always something fateful about the images and symbols that arise from it. "Perhaps—who knows?—these eternal images are what men mean by fate."[15]

[15] *Two Essays,* p. 107.

LIST OF WORKS CITED

I. WORKS OF C. G. JUNG

[For a revised (as of 1975) list of the Collected Works, see following page 230.]

In this volume, the edition now in process of the Collected Works of C. G. Jung is used, insofar as possible, for citations of his writings. (See list at the end of the book.) For works not yet published in that edition, reference is made to currently available versions, and the projected Collected Works version is cited in brackets with volume number starred.

Aion: Researches into the Phenomenology of the Self. Collected Works, 9, ii.

"Analytical Psychology and *Weltanschauung*." In Collected Works, 8.

"Answer to Job." In Collected Works, 11.

"The Archetypes of the Collective Unconscious." In Collected Works, 9, i.

"Die Bedeutung der Psychologie für die Gegenwart," in *Wirklichkeit der Seele*, q.v. ["The Meaning of Psychology for Modern Man," in Collected Works, *10.]

Commentary on "The Secret of the Golden Flower." In WILHELM, *The Secret of the Golden Flower*, q.v. in Part II. [In Collected Works, *13.]

"Concerning Mandala Symbolism." In Collected Works, 9, i.

"Concerning Rebirth." In Collected Works, 9, i.

"Concerning the Archetypes, with Special Reference to the Anima Concept." In Collected Works, 9, i.

Contributions to Analytical Psychology. Translated by H. G. and C. F. Baynes. London and New York, 1928.

Essays on a Science of Mythology (with C. KERÉNYI). Translated by R. F. C. Hull. New York (Bollingen Series XXII), 1949. (London, 1950, titled *An Introduction to a Science of Mythology*.)

ETH Lectures, 1938/39. Notes of a seminar given by Jung in German at the Eidgenössiche Technische Hochschule (Federal Polytechnical Institute), Zurich. Privately mimeographed.

"Instinct and the Unconscious." In Collected Works, 8.

The Interpretation of Nature and the Psyche (with W. PAULI). Translated by R. F. C. Hull and Priscilla Silz. New York (Bollingen Series LI) and London, 1955.

Introduction to: ESTHER HARDING. *Woman's Mysteries.* 2nd edn., New York, 1955.

Introduction to: W. M. KRANEFELDT. *Secret Ways of the Mind.* Translated by Ralph M. Eaton. London, 1934.

"Introduction to Wickes's 'Analyse der Kinderseele.'" In Collected Works, 17.

"Mind and Earth." In *Contributions to Analytical Psychology,* q.v. [In Collected Works, *10.]

Modern Man in Search of a Soul. Translated by W. S. Dell and C. F. Baynes. London and New York, 1933. (Also in Harvest Books paperback edn.)

Mysterium Coniunctionis (with M.-L. VON FRANZ). Zurich, 1955-57. 3 vols. [Jung's part = Collected Works, *14.]

"The Nature of Dreams." In Collected Works, 8.

"On Psychic Energy." In Collected Works, 8.

"On the Nature of the Psyche." In Collected Works, 8.

"On the Psychogenesis of Schizophrenia," *Journal of Mental Science* (London), LXXXV (Sept., 1939), 999-1011. [In Collected Works, *3.]

"On the Psychology of the Unconscious." In Collected Works, 7.

"On the Relation of Analytical Psychology to the Poetic Art." In *Contributions to Analytical Psychology,* q.v. [In Collected Works, *15.]

"Paracelsus als geistige Erscheinung." In: *Paracelsica.* Zurich, 1942. ["Paracelsus as a Spiritual Phenomenon," in Collected Works, *13.]

"The Paradigm of the Unicorn." In Collected Works, 12.

"The Phenomenology of the Spirit in Fairytales." In Collected Works, 9, i.

"Der philosophische Baum." In *Von den Wurzeln des Bewusstseins,* q.v. ["The 'Arbor philosophica,'" in Collected Works, *13.]

The Practice of Psychotherapy. Collected Works, 16.

"A Psychological Approach to the Dogma of the Trinity." In Collected Works, 11.

"The Psychological Aspects of the Kore." In Collected Works, 9, i.

"The Psychological Aspects of the Mother Archetype." In Collected Works, 9, i.

"Psychological Commentary on 'The Tibetan Book of the Dead.' " In Collected Works, 11. (See also EVANS-WENTZ, in Part II.)

"The Psychological Foundations of Belief in Spirits." In Collected Works, 8.

"A Psychological Theory of Types." In Modern Man in Search of a Soul, q.v. [In Collected Works, *6.]

Psychological Types. Translated by H. G. Baynes. London and New York, 1923. [In Collected Works, *6.]

Die Psychologie der unbewussten Prozesse. Zurich, 1917.

Psychology and Alchemy. Collected Works, 12.

"Psychology and Literature." In Modern Man in Search of a Soul, q.v. [In Collected Works, *15.]

"Psychology and Religion." In Collected Works, 11.

Psychology and Religion: West and East. Collected Works, 11.

The Psychology of Dementia Praecox. Translated by A. A. Brill. (Nervous and Mental Disease Monograph Series, 3.) New York and Washington, 1936. [In Collected Works, *3.]

"The Psychology of the Child Archetype." In Collected Works, 9, i.

"Psychology of the Transference." In Collected Works, 16.

"The Relations between the Ego and the Unconscious." In Collected Works, 7.

"A Review of the Complex Theory." In Collected Works, 8.

Seelenprobleme der Gegenwart. Zurich, 1946 (orig., 1931).

"The Soul and Death." In Collected Works, 8.

"Spirit and Life." In Collected Works, 8.

Studies in Word Association (with others). Translated by
M. D. Eder. London, 1918; New York, 1919. [In Collected
Works, *2.]

"A Study in the Process of Individuation." In Collected
Works, 9, i.

Symbolik des Geistes. Zurich, 1948.

Symbols of Transformation. Collected Works, 5.

"Synchronicity: An Acausal Connecting Principle." In Collected Works, 8.

"Transformation Symbolism in the Mass." In Collected
Works, 11.

Two Essays on Analytical Psychology. Collected Works, 7.

"Über den Archetypus, mit besonderer Berücksichtigung des
Animabegriffes," *Zentralblatt für Psychotherapie und ihre
Grenzgebiete* (Leipzig), IX (1936): 5, 264. [Rev. as "Con-
cerning the Archetypes," q.v.]

Über psychische Energetik und das Wesen der Träume.
Zurich, 1948.

"Die Visionen des Zosimos." In *Von den Wurzeln des Bewusstseins,* q.v. ["Some Observations on the Visions of
Zosimos," in Collected Works, *13.]

Wandlungen und Symbole der Libido. Leipzig and Vienna,
1912.

Von den Wurzeln des Bewusstseins. Zurich, 1954.

Wirklichkeit der Seele. Zurich, 1934.

"Zur gegenwärtigen Lage der Psychotherapie," *Zentralblatt
für Psychotherapie und ihre Grenzgebiete* (Leipzig), VII
(1934): 2. ["The State of Psychotherapy Today," in Collected Works, *10.]

II. WORKS OF OTHERS

ALLENDY, RENÉ FÉLIX. *Le Symbolisme des nombres.* Paris, 1948.

ALVERDES, F. "Die Wirksamkeit von Archetypen in den Instinkthandlungen der Tiere," *Zoologischer Anzeiger* (Leipzig), CXIX (1939).

AVALON, ARTHUR (pseud. of Sir John Woodroffe), ed. and tr. *The Serpent Power.* 3rd rev. edn., Madras and London, 1931.

BACHOFEN, J. J. *Versuch über die Gräbersymbolik der Alten.* Basel, 1859. See also his *Gesammelte Werke,* Vol. IV, Basel, 1954; and selections in: *Mutterrecht und Urreligion,* ed. Rudolf Marx (Kröners Taschenausgabe), Stuttgart, 1954.

BASH, K. W. "Gestalt, Symbol und Archetypus," *Schweizerische Zeitschrift für Psychologie* (Bern), V (1946): 2, 127-38.

Bible. Authorized ("King James") Version (abbr. AV).

BILZ, R. "Die anankastische Selbstregulation in Lebenskrisen," *Der Nervenarzt* (Berlin), No. 10 (Oct., 1954).

BLEULER, MANFRED. "Forschungen und Begriffswandlungen in der Schizophrenielehre 1941-1950," *Fortschritte der Neurologie, Psychiatrie und ihrer Grenzgebiete* (Leipzig), XIX (1951): 9-10, 385-452.

BOSS, MEDARD. *Der Traum und seine Auslegung.* Bern, 1953.

BOVET, THÉODORE. *Die Ganzheit der Person in der ärztlichen Praxis.* Zurich and Leipzig, 1940.

BUCKLAND, A. W. "Four as a Sacred Number," *Journal of the Anthropological Institute of Great Britain* (London), XXV (1896).

BUDGE, SIR E. A. WALLIS. *The Gods of the Egyptians.* London, 1904. 2 vols.

BURCKHARDT, JAKOB. *Briefe an Albert Brenner.* 2nd edn., Basel, 1918.

CARTARI, VINCENZO. *Le Imagini de i dei de gli antichi.* Lyons, 1581.

205

CARUS, KARL GUSTAV. *Symbolik der menschlichen Gestalt.* Leipzig, 1853.

CASSIRER, ERNST. *An Essay on Man.* New Haven and London, 1944.

————. *Philosophie der symbolischen Formen.* Berlin, 1923-29. 3 vols. Translation by Ralph Manheim: *The Philosophy of Symbolic Forms.* New Haven, 1953-57. 3 vols.

Corpus Hermeticum. See SCOTT.

CREUZER, FRIEDRICH. *Symbolik und Mythologie der alten Völker.* Leipzig and Darmstadt, 1810-23. 6 vols.

DIONYSIUS THE AREOPAGITE. *On the Divine Names and the Mystical Theology.* Translated by C. E. Rolt. (Translations of Christian Literature.) London and New York, 1920.

DOERING, OSKAR. *Christliche Symbole.* Freiburg i. B., 1933.

ELIADE, MIRCEA. *The Myth of the Eternal Return.* Translated by Willard R. Trask. New York (Bollingen Series XLVI) and London, 1955.

ELLIOT SMITH, SIR GRAFTON. See SMITH.

ENDRES, FRANZ CARL. *Die Zahl in Mystik und Glauben der Kulturvölker.* Zurich and Leipzig, 1935.

ERKES, EDUARD, "Strohhund und Regendrache," *Artibus Asiae* (Leipzig), IV (1930), 205-12.

EVANS-WENTZ, W. Y. *The Tibetan Book of the Dead.* With a psychological commentary by C. G. Jung. 3rd edn., London, 1957.

[FIERZ-DAVID, LINDA.] *The Dream of Poliphilo.* Related and interpreted by Linda Fierz-David. Translated by Mary Hottinger. (Bollingen Series XXV.) New York, 1950.

FORDHAM, FRIEDA. *An Introduction to Jung's Psychology.* (Penguin Books.) London and Baltimore, 1953.

FRANZ, MARIE-LOUISE VON. "Der Traum des Descartes." In: *Zeitlose Dokumente der Seele.* (Studien aus dem C. G. Jung-Institut III.) Zurich, 1952.

FREUD, SIGMUND. *From the History of an Infantile Neurosis.* In: *An Infantile Neurosis and Other Works.* (Standard Edition of the Complete Psychological Works, translated by James Strachey and others, XVII.) London, 1955.

———. *The Interpretation of Dreams*. (Standard Edition of the Complete Psychological Works, translated by James Strachey and others, IV-V.) London, 1953. Also in: *The Basic Writings of Sigmund Freud*. (Modern Library Giant.) New York, 1938.

———. "The Occurrence in Dreams of Material from Fairy Tales." In: *Collected Papers*, IV. London, 1925.

———. *Psychopathology of Everyday Life*. Translated by A. A. Brill. London, 1914. Also in: *The Basic Writings of Sigmund Freud*. (Modern Library Giant.) New York, 1938.

FROBENIUS, LEO. *Das Zeitalter des Sonnengottes*. Berlin, 1904.

FROMM, ERICH. *The Forgotten Language*. New York [1951] and London, 1952.

FUHRMANN, ERNST. *Das Tier in der Religion*. Munich, 1922.

GOETHE, JOHANN WOLFGANG VON. *Goethe's Theory of Colours*. Translated by C. L. Eastlake. London, 1840.

———. *Maximen und Reflexionen*. Gedenkausgabe, vol. 9. Zurich, 1949.

GRIMM, JACOB AND WILHELM. *Grimm's Fairy Tales*. Translated by Margaret Hunt, revised by James Stern. New York and London, 1944.

GUNKEL, JOHN FRIEDRICH HERMANN. *Schöpfung und Chaos in Urzeit und Endzeit*. Göttingen, 1895.

Handwörterbuch des Deutschen Aberglaubens. Edited by Hanns Bächtold-Stäubli. Berlin and Leipzig, 1927-42.

HEDIGER, HENRI. "Bemerkungen zum Raum-Zeit-System der Tiere," *Schweizerische Zeitschrift für Psychologie und ihre Anwendung* (Bern), V (1946): 4.

HENTZE, CARL. *Tod, Auferstehung, Weltordnung*. Zurich, 1955.

HESSE, RICHARD. *Tiergeographie auf ökologischer Grundlage*. Jena, 1924. (*Ecological Animal Geography*. An authorized edn., rewritten and revised by W. C. Adler and Karl P. Schmidt. 2nd edn., New York, 1951.)

HOMER. *The Iliad: The Story of Achilles*. Translated by W. H. D. Rouse. London and New York, 1938.

HOPPER, VINCENT FOSTER. *Medieval Number Symbolism.* New York, 1938.

HUXLEY, ALDOUS. *The Devils of Loudun.* New York and London, 1952.

IRENAEUS, SAINT. *Five Books of Irenaeus against Heresies.* Translated by John Keble. (Library of Fathers of the Holy Catholic Church). Oxford, 1872.

JACOBI, JOLANDE. "Der Beitrag Jungs zur Psychologie des Kindes," *Der Psychologe* (Schwarzenburg-Bern), II (1950): 7/8.

———. "Ich und Selbst in der Kinderzeichnung," *Schweizerische Zeitschrift für Psychologie und ihre Anwendung* (Bern), XII (1953): 1.

———. *The Psychology of C. G. Jung.* Translated by K. W. Bash. 2nd edn., London and New Haven, 1951. (These are different printings, therefore double page refs. are given. A new translation by Ralph Manheim is in preparation.)

JAFFÉ, ANIELA. "Bilder und Symbole aus E. T. A. Hoffmanns Märchen 'Der Goldne Topf.' " In: C. G. JUNG. *Gestaltungen des Unbewussten.* Zurich, 1950.

JUNG, CARL GUSTAV. See Part I of the List of Works Cited.

JUSTIN MARTYR, SAINT. *Apology.* In: *The Writings of Justin Martyr and Athenagoras.* Translated by Marcus Dods, George Reith, and B. P. Pratten. (Ante-Nicene Christian Library, 2.) Edinburgh, 1867.

KAILA, E. "Die Reaktionen des Säuglings auf das menschliche Gesicht," *Annuarium Universitatis Aboensis* (Turku, Finland), XVII (1952).

KANT, IMMANUEL. *The Critique of Judgement.* Translated with analytical indexes by James Creed Meredith. Oxford, 1952.

KATZ, DAVID. *Gestalt Psychology, Its Nature and Significance.* Translated by Robert Tyson. New York, 1950; London, 1951. (Orig., Basel, 1914.)

KERÉNYI, KARL. "Das Geheimnis der Pythia." In: *Apollon.* Zurich, 1953.

———. *The Gods of the Greeks.* Translated by Norman Cameron. London and New York, 1951.

————. *Labyrinth-Studien*. (Albae Vigiliae, XV.) Amsterdam, 1943.

————. *Töchter der Sonne*. Zurich, 1944.

———— and C. G. JUNG. *Essays on a Science of Mythology*. See Part I.

———— and L. M. LANCKORONSKI. *Der Mythos der Hellenen*. Amsterdam and Leipzig. 1941.

Kleines Lexikon der Antike. Bern, 1950.

KÜKELHAUS, HUGO. *Urzahl und Gebärde*. Berlin, 1934.

KÜSTER, ERICH. *Die Schlange in der griechischen Kunst und Religion*. (Religionsgeschichtliche Versuche und Vorarbeiten. . . , edited by Richard Wünsche and Ludwig Deubner, XIII, 2.) Giessen, 1913.

LEISEGANG, HANS. *Die Gnosis*. (Kröners Taschenausgabe.) Leipzig, 1924.

LORENZ, KONRAD. "Die angeborenen Formen möglicher Erfahrung," *Zeitschrift für Tierpsychologie* (Berlin), V (1943).

MEIER, C. A. *Antike Inkubation und moderne Psychotherapie*. (Studien aus dem C. G. Jung-Institut, I.) Zurich, 1949.

Meyers Konversations-Lexikon. Leipzig, 1905-13. 24 vols.

NEUMANN, ERICH. *The Great Mother*. Translated by Ralph Manheim. New York (Bollingen Series XLVII) and London, 1955.

————. *The Origins and History of Consciousness*. Translated by R. F. C. Hull. New York (Bollingen Series XLII) and London, 1954.

————. *Zur Psychologie des Weiblichen*. (Umkreisung der Mitte, II.) Zurich, 1953.

The New Schaff-Herzog Encyclopedia of Religious Knowledge. Edited by Samuel Macaulay Jackson. London, 1908-14. 13 vols.

NINCK, MARTIN. *Wodan und germanischer Schicksalsglaube*. Jena, 1935.

NOVALIS, pseud. (Friedrich von Hardenberg). *Heinrich von Ofterdingen*. 1802.

PANETH, LUDWIG. *Zahlensymbolik im Unbewussten*. Zurich, 1952.

PAULI, W. "The Influence of Archetypal Ideas on the Scientific Theories of Kepler." See Part I: *The Interpretation of Nature and the Psyche*, which contains it.

PHILIPPSON, PAULA. *Untersuchungen über den griechischen Mythos*. Zurich, 1944.

PIAGET, JEAN. *Play, Dreams and Imitation in Childhood*. Translated by C. Gattegno and F. M. Hodgson. London and New York, 1951. (Orig., Neuchâtel and Paris, 1945.)

PLUTARCH. "The E at Delphi." In: *Moralia*. With an English translation by F. C. Babbitt. (Loeb Classical Library.) London and New York, 1927ff. 14 vols. (Vol. 5, pp. 198-253.)

———. "Isis and Osiris." In ibid. (Pp. 6-191.)

PORTMANN, ADOLF. "Das Problem der Urbilder in biologischer Sicht," *Eranos-Jahrbuch* (Zurich), XVIII (1950: special volume for Jung's 75th birthday).

———. "Riten der Tiere," *Eranos-Jahrbuch*, XIX (1950).

PRELLER, LUDWIG. *Griechische Mythologie*. Berlin, 1921. 2 vols.

SCHLESINGER, M. *Geschichte des Symbols*. Berlin, 1912. Supplement, 1930.

SCHMITT, PAUL. "Archetypisches bei Augustin und Goethe," *Eranos Jahrbuch* (Zurich), XII (1945: special volume for Jung's 70th birthday).

SCHNEIDER, E. "Zur Psychologie des Unbewussten," *Schweizerische Zeitschrift für Psychologie* (Zurich), XI (1952): 2.

SCHNEIDER, KARL CAMILLO. "Tierpsychologie." In: *Einführung in die neuere Psychologie*. Edited by Emil Saupe-Halle. (Handbücher der neueren Erziehungswisse, 3.) Vienna, 1931.

SCOTT, WALTER, ed. and tr. *Hermetica*. Oxford, 1924-36. 4 vols.

SCHREBER, DANIEL P. *Memoirs of My Nervous Illness*. (Psychiatric Monograph Series, 1.) Translated by Ida Macalpine and Richard A. Hunter. London, 1955. (Orig., 1903.)

SCHUBERT, GOTTHILF HEINRICH VON. *Die Symbolik des Traumes*. Leipzig, 1840.

SILBERER, HERBERT. *Durch Tod zum Leben.* (Beiträge zur Geschichte der neueren Mystik und Magie, 4.) Leipzig, 1915.

————. *Problems of Mysticism and Its Symbolism.* Translated by Smith Ely Jelliffe. New York, 1915. (Orig., 1914.)

SINGER, H. F. *Der blaue Montag.* Mainz, 1917.

SMITH, SIR GRAFTON ELLIOT. *The Evolution of the Dragon.* Manchester, 1919.

SPITZ, RENÉ ARPAD. *The Smiling Response.* (Genetic Psychology Monographs, 34.) Provincetown, Mass., 1946.

STAUDENMAIER, LUDWIG. *Die Magie als experimentelle Naturwissenschaft.* Leipzig, 1912.

STIRNIMANN, F. *Psychologie des neugeborenen Kindes.* Zurich, 1940.

SZONDI, LIPOT. *Ichanalyse.* Bern and Stuttgart, 1956.

URBAN, WILBUR MARSHALL. *Language and Reality: The Philosophy and the Principles of Symbolism.* New York and London, 1939.

ÜXKÜLL, JAKOB VON. *Umwelt und Innenwelt der Tiere.* Berlin, 1909.

WARREN, HOWARD CROSBY, ed. *Dictionary of Psychology.* New York, 1934; London, 1935.

WEIS, A. "Christliche Symbolik." Unpublished lecture, 1952.

WICKES, FRANCES G. *Analyse der Kinderseele.* Stuttgart, 1951. (Orig.: *The Inner World of Childhood.* New York, 1927.)

[WILHELM, RICHARD.] *The Secret of the Golden Flower: a Chinese Book of Life.* Translated and explained by Richard Wilhelm, with a European commentary by C. G. Jung. Translated into English by Cary F. Baynes. London and New York, 1931.

ZELLER, EDUARD. *Die Philosophie der Griechen in ihrer geschichtlichen Entwicklung dargestellt.* Tübingen, 1856. 3 vols. (*A History of Greek Philosophy.* . . . Translated by S. F. Alleyne, London, 1881. 2 vols.)

INDEX

INDEX

58; legend and fairytale, 33;
 migration of, 33
music, 109f
mysticism, Christian, square in,
 169
mystics, 106, 177
myth(s), 27, 76, 118, 130, 137,
 180ff; bad animal in, 156;
 creation, 180, 182f; of dying
 hero, 46; living and lived, 67;
 parallels in, 109; of solar
 hero, 47, 147, 183; time in,
 185; whale-dragon, 177, 180,
 187
mythologem(s), 33, 67, 106n,
 108ff, 120
mythology(-ies): archetypes
 and, 109; individual, 109;
 see also Babylonian mythology;
 Egyptian mythology; Greek
 mythology

N

Naassenes, 149
Naga serpents, 153
names, changing of, 67
Nekyia, 156, 180, 186
nest building, 41
Neumann, Erich, 146n
"neuralgic points," 20
neurosis, 18, 27, 28ff, 72; and
 psychosis, distinction, 28; *see
 also* compulsion neurosis
neurotics: participation in, 17;
 and symbols, 93f
New Testament, 157; *see also*
 Gospels *and names of specific
 books*
new year, 178n
Nibelungs, 156
Nicodemus, 100
night, as symbol, 91
night sea journey, 179ff, 183,
 184, 185ff
nigredo, 157
Niklaus von der Flüe, St., 104f
Nile floods, 147

Ninck, Martin, 147n
Noah's ark, 158, 184
nodal points, 24f, 26, 27, 33,
 35, 52, 116, 119, 121
North Pole, 184
Nous, 159n
Novalis, 164n
nuclear element, in complex, 8f,
 24, 26, 121
number symbolism, 173
numbers: archetypal foundation
 of, 115n; even, 146; *see also*
 one; four; five
Numbers, Book of, 157n, 159n
numinosity: of archetypes, 56f,
 112; of complexes, 11
Nun, 144
Nut, 184

O

obsessions, 12
octopus, 41, 152
Odyssey, 180n
ogre, 155
Old Testament, 24, 145; *see also
 names of specific books*
"One," the, 170ff; separation
 into four, 173
one, the number, as masculine,
 173
Ophites, 149
opposites: confrontation of,
 115; pairs of, archetype as
 reconciling, 95; —, in symbols
 and complexes, 123;
 primordial, conflict of, 142;
 —, unity of, 56; tension of,
 143; union of, through
 symbol, 98f
opus: alchemical, 146, 154,
 168; *circulare,* 185
order: archetype of, 115n;
 mandalas as symbols of, 193n
orderedness, acausal, 64
Osiris, 147, 182, 183
Oyster Bay tribe, 182

The Collected Works of C. G. Jung

Editors: Sir Herbert Read, Michael Fordham, and Gerhard Adler; executive editor, William McGuire. Translated by R.F.C. Hull, except where noted.

(*continued*)

(*continued*)

(continued)

(*continued*)

Child Development and Education (1928)
Analytical Psychology and Education: Three Lectures (1926/1946)
The Gifted Child (1943)
The Significance of the Unconscious in Individual Education (1928)
The Development of Personality (1934)
Marriage as a Psychological Relationship (1925)

18. THE SYMBOLIC LIFE (1954)
Translated by R.F.C. Hull and others
Miscellaneous Writings

19. COMPLETE BIBLIOGRAPHY OF C. G. JUNG'S WRITINGS
(1976; 2d ed., 1992)

20. GENERAL INDEX OF THE COLLECTED WORKS (1979)

THE ZOFINGIA LECTURES (1983)
Supplementary Volume A to the Collected Works.
Edited by William McGuire, translated by
Jan van Heurck, introduction by
Marie-Louise von Franz

PSYCHOLOGY OF THE UNCONSCIOUS ([1912] 1992)
A STUDY OF THE TRANSFORMATIONS AND SYMBOLISMS OF THE LIBIDO.
A CONTRIBUTION TO THE HISTORY OF THE EVOLUTION OF THOUGHT
Supplementary Volume B to the Collected Works.
Translated by Beatrice M. Hinkle,
introduction by William McGuire

Related Publications

THE BASIC WRITINGS OF C. G. JUNG
Selected and introduced by Violet S. de Laszlo

PSYCHE AND SYMBOL
Selected and introduced by Violet S. de Laszlo

C. G. JUNG: LETTERS
Selected and edited by Gerhard Adler, in collaboration with Aniela Jaffé.
Translations from the German by R.F.C. Hull
VOL. 1: 1906–1950
VOL. 2: 1951–1961

THE FREUD / JUNG LETTERS
Edited by William McGuire, translated by
Ralph Manheim and R.F.C. Hull

C. G. JUNG SPEAKING: Interviews and Encounters
Edited by William McGuire and R.F.C. Hull

C. G. JUNG: Word and Image
Edited by Aniela Jaffé

THE ESSENTIAL JUNG
Selected and introduced by Anthony Storr

THE GNOSTIC JUNG
Selected and introduced by Robert A. Segal

Notes to C. G. Jung's Seminars

DREAM ANALYSIS ([1928–30] 1984)
Edited by William McGuire

NIETZSCHE'S *ZARATHUSTRA* ([1934–39] 1988)
Edited by James L. Jarrett (2 vols.)

ANALYTICAL PSYCHOLOGY ([1925] 1989)
Edited by William McGuire

THE PSYCHOLOGY OF KUNDALINI YOGA ([1932] 1996)
Edited by Sonu Shamdasani

INTERPRETATION OF VISIONS ([1930–34] 1997)
Edited by Claire Douglas

JOLANDE JACOBI

Jolande Jacobi was born Jolan Székacs in Budapest on March 25, 1890, daughter of the senator and privy councillor Antal Székacs. In 1909, she married Dr. Andor Jacobi, a distinguished Hungarian lawyer, and in 1919, for political reasons, they emigrated to Vienna. There she became active in cultural and social affairs, and as executive vice-president of the Austrian Kulturbund (cultural society) she invited many European writers, scientists, and political figures—including C. G. Jung—to speak in Vienna, and organized exhibitions of the work of famous painters and sculptors. In 1934, after her two sons had finished their schooling, Jolan Jacobi began graduate study in psychology at Vienna University, working chiefly under Karl and Charlotte Bühler, and in 1938 she earned the Ph.D. The same year, *Anschluss* brought Austria under the Nazi yoke and she fled to Switzerland, destitute, to begin a new life. (She later adopted the spelling Jolande for her given name.)

In Zurich, Dr. Jacobi began her studies and analysis with C. G. Jung, and within a few years she became one of the leading interpreters of his school of analytical psychology. She is credited with bringing Jungian psychology into an organized system, particularly through her book *The Psychology of C. G. Jung* (Yale), which has had numerous German and English editions and has been translated into nine languages. She was one of the founders and directors of the C. G. Jung Institute in Zurich, and she taught and lectured there and at the Institute for Applied Psychology, the Volkshochschule, and Zurich University, as well as in other European countries, in England, and in the United States. She carried on research at the Zürichberg Clinic, specializing in art therapy. Until the end of her long life she conducted an analytic practice in German, Hungarian, and English. She was a member of the Swiss Society of Catholic Psychoanalysts and many other organizations.

Jolande Jacobi published more than one hundred papers and contributed the following books in translation to Bollingen Series: *C. G. Jung: Psychological Reflections: An Anthology of His Writings*, which she edited (originally 1953; new edition, embracing Jung's works to the end of his life, 1970, in collaboration with R.F.C. Hull); *Paracelsus: Selected Writings*, which she had translated into modern German, edited, and introduced; and her original study *Complex / Archetype / Symbol in the Psychology of C. G. Jung*. Her other works include *The Way of Individuation* and untranslated books on problems of women and marriage, the paintings and drawings of analytic patients, and the archetype of the psychological mask.

The Austrian Government awarded her the Knight's Cross of the Order of Merit in 1935 and the Cross of Honor for Science and Art in 1972.

Jolande Jacobi died suddenly in Zurich on April 1, 1973, in the midst of her work toward organizing an exhibition, under the auspices of the City of Zurich, in honor of C. G. Jung's one hundredth birthday in 1975.